COLLECTED POEMS

by the same author

poetry
MAKING COCOA FOR KINGSLEY AMIS
THE RIVER GIRL
SERIOUS CONCERNS
IF I DON'T KNOW
TWO CURES FOR LOVE: Selected Poems 1979–2006
FAMILY VALUES
CHRISTMAS POEMS
ANECDOTAL EVIDENCE
THE ORANGE AND OTHER POEMS

prose
LIFE, LOVE AND THE ARCHERS:
Recollections, Reviews and Other Prose

for children
TWIDDLING YOUR THUMBS
GOING FOR A DRIVE

as editor
THE FUNNY SIDE: 101 Funny Poems
THE FABER BOOK OF BEDTIME STORIES
IS THAT THE NEW MOON?
THE ORCHARD BOOK OF FUNNY POEMS
HEAVEN ON EARTH: 101 Happy Poems
GEORGE HERBERT: A Selection

WENDY COPE
COLLECTED POEMS

faber

First published in 2024
by Faber & Faber Ltd
The Bindery, 51 Hatton Garden
London, EC1N 8HN

Typeset by Hamish Ironside
Printed by Marquis, Toronto, Canada

All rights reserved
© Wendy Cope, 2024

The right of Wendy Cope to be identified as author of this work
has been asserted in accordance with Section 77 of the Copyright,
Designs and Patents Act 1988

A CIP record for this book
is available from the British Library

ISBN 978–0–571–38325–2

Printed in Canada on FSC® certified paper in line with our continuing commitment
to ethical business practices, sustainability and the environment.
For further information see faber.co.uk/environmental-policy.

2 4 6 8 10 9 7 5 3 1

To Lachlan, with love

CONTENTS

Introductory Note xix

MAKING COCOA FOR KINGSLEY AMIS (1986)
— I —

Engineers' Corner	5
All-Purpose Poem for State Occasions	6
A Policeman's Lot	7
Reading Scheme	9
A Nursery Rhyme *(as it might have been written by William Wordsworth)*	10
A Nursery Rhyme *(as it might have been written by T. S. Eliot)*	11
Waste Land Limericks	12
Triolet	14
Emily Dickinson	15
Proverbial Ballade	16
Advertisement	18
Lonely Hearts	19
On Finding an Old Photograph	20
Tich Miller	21
At 3 a.m.	22
From June to December	23
My Lover	28
Rondeau Redoublé	31
Message	32
Giving Up Smoking	33
Manifesto	34

— II —

Mr Strugnell	37
Budgie Finds His Voice	39
Usquebaugh	40
The Lavatory Attendant	41
E Pericoloso Sporgersi	42
Duffa Rex	43
Strugnell in Liverpool	44
Narrative	46
God and the Jolly Bored Bog-Mouse	47
from Strugnell's Sonnets	
(i) 'The expense of spirits'	48
(ii) 'Not from the stars'	49
(iii) 'My glass shall not'	50
(iv) 'Not only marble'	51
(v) 'How like a sprinter'	52
(vi) 'Let me not'	53
(vii) 'Indeed 'tis true'	54
from Strugnell's *Rubáiyát*	55
Strugnell's Haiku	57
Notes on the Parodies in Section II	58

— III —

Making Cocoa for Kingsley Amis	61

UNCOLLECTED POEMS (1973–1985)

Depression	65
Going Away	66
The Journey	67
Score	68
Word-Watching	69
Thaw	70
Sunset at Widemouth Bay	71

Grandmother	72
Sisters	73
My Favourite Game	75
Current Affairs	76
Revenge	77
from Strugnell's Sonnets	
(viii) 'When in disgrace'	79
(ix) 'Oh, never say'	80
(x) 'How sober was I'	81
(xi) 'Shall I compare'	82
Strugnell's Bargain	83
A Shorter Version of Wordsworth's Immortality Ode	84
Ballad of an Office Romance	85

THE RIVER GIRL (1991)

The River Girl	91

SERIOUS CONCERNS (1992)

Flowers	145
Defining the Problem	146
The Aerial	147
The Orange	148
Some More Light Verse	149
As Sweet	150
Loss	151
Two Cures for Love	152
Favourite	153
Another Unfortunate Choice	154
Letter	155
Nine-Line Triolet	156
Magnetic	157
On a Country Bus	158
After the Lunch	159

In the Rhine Valley	160
Valentine	161
Faint Praise	162
I Worry	163
So Much Depends	164
A Christmas Poem	165
The New Regime	166
New Season	167
Legacy	168
Names	169
For My Sister, Emigrating	170
Leaving	171
The Uncertainty of the Poet	172
Poem Composed in Santa Barbara	173
The Poet's Song	174
Tumps	176
The Cricketing Versions	177
Another Christmas Poem	179
19th Christmas Poem	180
Reflections on a Royalty Statement	182
An Argument with Wordsworth	184
Variation on Belloc's 'Fatigue'	185
Bloody Men	186
Men and Their Boring Arguments	187
Noises in the Night	188
Advice to Young Women	189
Variation on a Lennon and McCartney Song	190
Exchange of Letters	191
A Green Song	193
The Concerned Adolescent	194
Goldfish Nation	196
Roger Bear's Football Poems	199
Roger Bear's Philosophical Pantoum	200
Strugnell's Evangelical Songs	202
from Strugnell Lunaire	205

the homeless hammer	206
Ahead of My Time	
Clouds	207
Perplexity	207
Weltschmerz	207
Quartet for Four Beer-drinkers	208
English Weather	209
Serious Concerns	210
Kindness to Animals	211
Does She Like Word Games?	212

UNCOLLECTED POEMS (1986–1991)

Lauda	215
Sonnet ('A German dictionary on my knee')	216
You and I	217
In a Clifftop Shelter at Falmouth	218
Closing the Anthology	219
In Demand	220
Postcard Poem	221
A Contented Poem	222
Where Do You Get Your Ideas From?	223
On Learning the Correct Pronunciation of the Name of a Poetic Form	224

IF I DON'T KNOW (2001)

— I —

By the Round Pond	229
The Christmas Life	230
30th December	231
If I Don't Know	232
Haiku: Looking Out of the Back Bedroom Window without My Glasses	233
Idyll	234

Being Boring	235
Fireworks Poems	236
Timekeeping	237
Song	238
On a Train	240
Present	241
Postcards	242
Sonnet of '68	243
A Word before Sleep	244
After Prague	245
The Sitter	246
Les Vacances	247
Dead Sheep Poem	248
The Lyric Poet	249
A Mystery	250
Reading Berryman's Dream Songs at the Writers' Retreat	251
The Squirrel and the Crow	252
John Clare	255
An Ending	256
Poem from a Colour Chart of House Paints	257
Greek Island Triolets	259
The Ted Williams Villanelle	261
He Tells Her	262
What I Think	263
The Sorrow of Socks	264
The Stickleback Song	265
Stress	267
A Hampshire Disaster	268
A Poem on the Theme of Humour	269
A Reading	270
How to Deal with the Press	271
Traditional Prize County Pigs	272
Elegy for the Northern Wey	275
Tulips	276

— II —

The Teacher's Tale   279

UNCOLLECTED POEMS (1992–2000)

At Cathedral Mattins	303
Cathedral Limerick	304
Mozart in the Shopping Centre	305
Autumn Haiku	306
Poem for L	307
Egg Cookery	308
Riddle	309
The South Bank Poetry Library, London	310
Team Spirit	311
Pianists	312
Strugnell's Royal Wedding Poem	313
Thirteen Ways of Curing a Headache	314

from TWO CURES FOR LOVE: SELECTED POEMS 1979–2006 (2008)

An Attempt at Unrhymed Verse	317
Limerick ('A talented young chimpanzee')	318

FAMILY VALUES (2011)

A Christmas Song	321
Christmas Ornaments	322
Cathedral Carol Service	323
O Come, All Ye Faithful	324
Differences of Opinion	325
Sunday Morning	327
You're Not Allowed	328
Daily Help	329
Boarders	332

Omo	334
The Women's Merchant Navy	335
The Africans	337
Uncle Bill	338
Brahms Cradle Song	339
Greydawn	340
At Stafford Services	341
At the Poetry Conference	342
The Health Scare	343
Sixty-one	344
Keep Saying This	345
Once I'm Dead	346
My Funeral	347
Seeing You	348
Macedonia 1987	349
Dutch Portraits	350
Haiku ('A perfect white wine')	351
April	352
The Month of May	353
Lissadell	354
At Steep	355
A Villanelle for Hugo Williams	356
Two Ann(e)s	357
Special Needs	358
Old Boys' Day	359
Probably	360
Stars	361
An Anniversary Poem	362
Spared	363
Another Valentine	364

~

from The Audience	
Prologue: The Performers	367

The Cougher	369
The Traditionalist	370
The Radical	371
The Critic	372
First Date: She	373
First Date: He	374
The Widow	375
A Rehearsal	376

from An ABC of the BBC

The Archers and Adultery	377
Digital and Interactive	378
Football	379
The Middle Classes	380
Quizzes	381
Unbearable	382
X-rated	383
Closedown	384

UNCOLLECTED POEMS (2001–2009)

Forty-seven Words	387
After Heine	
Ich glaub nicht an den Himmel	388
Ich hab im Traum geweinet	389
Herz, mein Herz, sei nicht beklommen	389
Sporty People	390
Travel Sonnet	391

from CHRISTMAS POEMS (2017)

Christmas Triolet	395
Motorway Music	396
Bethlehem	397

ANECDOTAL EVIDENCE (2018)

Evidence	401
The Damage to the Piano	402
Baggage	403
Orb	404
1952	405
Bags	406
Upheavals	408
Absent Friends	410
Reunion	412
An Afternoon	413
1972	414
Memorial	415
A Vow	416
To My Husband	417
Calculations	418
One Day	419
The Tree	420
Here We Are	421
Ely	422
March 2013	423
Haiku: Willows	424
Naga-Uta ('Clearest of clear days')	425
By the River	426
Shakespeare at School	427
The Marriage	428
On Sonnet 18	429
The Worst Row	430
My Father's Shakespeare	431
At New Place	432
Young Love	433
If It Be Now	434
In Memory of Max Adrian 1903–1973	435
On Sonnet 22	436

A Wreath for George Herbert	437
A Poem about Jesus	438
Little Donkey	439
Lantern Carol	440
Christmas Cards	441
In Memory of Dennis O'Driscoll	442
In Memory of a Psychoanalyst	444
A Little Tribute to John Cage	446
A Statue	447
Cento	448
Where's a Pied Piper When You Need One?	449
On a Photograph of the Archbishop of Canterbury	450
Men Talking	451
At 70	452
Health Advice	454
New Year	455
Tallis's Canon	456
Que Sera	457
Every	458

UNCOLLECTED POEMS (2010–2017)

Saint Hilda of Whitby: A Cantata	461
Teach Me	466
Translation	467
Haiku ('Silly butterfly')	468
On the Demise of Little Chef	469
Roy	470

UNCOLLECTED POEMS (2018–2023)

The Aunts	473
A Poem	474
On the Death of Archbishop Desmond Tutu	475

Naga-Uta ('Now I can't walk far')	476
The Beginning	477
The End	478

Acknowledgements 481
Index of Titles and First Lines 483

INTRODUCTORY NOTE

As I put this volume together, I trawled through a large number of my uncollected poems (i.e. poems that had not been included in any of my books). Some of them were written more than forty years ago. There was much dross and a few nice surprises.

Some of the uncollected poems had appeared in newspapers or magazines. Some had never been published anywhere. This book is their last chance to avoid being consigned to oblivion. With the help of three discerning readers – my husband Lachlan Mackinnon, my friend Rory Waterman and my editor Matthew Hollis – I have chosen the surviving poems. I thank those readers for their time and patience.

Each section of uncollected poems appears immediately after the collection the poems could have appeared in. The largest section is the earliest – 1973–1985 – because the poems had accumulated over a longer period of time, and because my then editor Craig Raine and I were very cautious in selecting the contents of my first book. The poems in the final uncollected section were written after the publication of *Anecdotal Evidence*.

This volume also includes my five published collections, plus an illustrated narrative poem, *The River Girl*. There are also some items from two compilations – *Two Cures for Love: Selected Poems* and *Christmas Poems*. Under those titles here you will find only the poems that don't also appear in one of my collections.

I have taken out a small handful of poems from my second book, *Serious Concerns*, and altered the order in which the poems appear. Where the other books are concerned, I have made only minor alterations.

My most recent book, *The Orange and Other Poems*,

doesn't feature here because all the poems in that compilation had already appeared in earlier collections and can be found in this volume.

Wendy Cope
May 2024

MAKING COCOA FOR
KINGSLEY AMIS

— 1986 —

I

Engineers' Corner

'Why isn't there an Engineers' Corner in Westminster Abbey? In Britain we've always made more fuss of a ballad than a blueprint . . . How many schoolchildren dream of becoming great engineers?'
         – Advertisement placed in The Times by the Engineering Council

We make more fuss of ballads than of blueprints –
That's why so many poets end up rich,
While engineers scrape by in cheerless garrets.
Who needs a bridge or dam? Who needs a ditch?

Whereas the person who can write a sonnet
Has got it made. It's always been the way,
For everybody knows that we need poems
And everybody reads them every day.

Yes, life is hard if you choose engineering –
You're sure to need another job as well;
You'll have to plan your projects in the evenings
Instead of going out. It must be hell.

While well-heeled poets ride around in Daimlers,
You'll burn the midnight oil to earn a crust,
With no hope of a statue in the Abbey,
With no hope, even, of a modest bust.

No wonder small boys dream of writing couplets
And spurn the bike, the lorry and the train.
There's far too much encouragement for poets –
That's why this country's going down the drain.

All-Purpose Poem for State Occasions

The nation rejoices or mourns
As this happy or sombre day dawns.
Our eyes will be wet
As we sit round the set,
Neglecting our flowerbeds and lawns.

As Her Majesty rides past the crowd
They'll be silent or cheer very loud
But whatever they do
It's undoubtedly true
That they'll feel patriotic and proud.

In Dundee and Penzance and Ealing
We're imbued with appropriate feeling:
We're British and loyal
And love every royal
And tonight we shall drink till we're reeling.

A Policeman's Lot

*'The progress of any writer is marked by those moments
when he manages to outwit his own inner police system.'*
— TED HUGHES

Oh, once I was a policeman young and merry
                                        (young and merry),
Controlling crowds and fighting petty crime (petty crime),
But now I work on matters literary (litererry)
And I am growing old before my time ('fore my time).
No, the imagination of a writer (of a writer)
Is not the sort of beat a chap would choose
                                        (chap would choose)
And they've assigned me a prolific blighter ('lific blighter) –
I'm patrolling the unconscious of Ted Hughes.

It's not the sort of beat a chap would choose
                                        (chap would choose) –
Patrolling the unconscious of Ted Hughes.

All our leave was cancelled in the lambing season
                                        (lambing season),
When bitter winter froze the drinking trough
                                        (drinking trough),
For our commander stated, with good reason
                                        (with good reason),
That that's the kind of thing that starts him off
                                        (starts him off).
But anything with four legs causes trouble (causes trouble) –
It's worse than organising several zoos (several zoos),
Not to mention mythic creatures in the rubble
                                        (in the rubble),
Patrolling the unconscious of Ted Hughes.

It's worse than organising several zoos (several zoos),
Patrolling the unconscious of Ted Hughes.

Although it's disagreeable and stressful (bull and stressful)
Attempting to avert poetic thought ('etic thought),
I could boast of times when I have been successful
                                           (been successful)
And conspiring compound epithets were caught
                                           ('thets were caught).
But the poetry statistics in this sector (in this sector)
Are enough to make a copper turn to booze (turn to booze)
And I do not think I'll make it to inspector (to inspector)
Patrolling the unconscious of Ted Hughes.

It's enough to make a copper turn to booze (turn to booze) –
Patrolling the unconscious of Ted Hughes.

after W. S. *Gilbert*

Reading Scheme

Here is Peter. Here is Jane. They like fun.
Jane has a big doll. Peter has a ball.
Look, Jane, look! Look at the dog! See him run!

Here is Mummy. She has baked a bun.
Here is the milkman. He has come to call.
Here is Peter. Here is Jane. They like fun.

Go Peter! Go Jane! Come, milkman, come!
The milkman likes Mummy. She likes them all.
Look, Jane, look! Look at the dog! See him run!

Here are the curtains. They shut out the sun.
Let us peep! On tiptoe Jane! You are small!
Here is Peter. Here is Jane. They like fun.

I hear a car, Jane. The milkman looks glum.
Here is Daddy in his car. Daddy is tall.
Look, Jane, look! Look at the dog! See him run!

Daddy looks very cross. Has he a gun?
Up milkman! Up milkman! Over the wall!
Here is Peter. Here is Jane. They like fun.
Look, Jane, look! Look at the dog! See him run!

A Nursery Rhyme

as it might have been written by William Wordsworth

The skylark and the jay sang loud and long,
The sun was calm and bright, the air was sweet,
When all at once I heard above the throng
Of jocund birds a single plaintive bleat.

And, turning, saw, as one sees in a dream,
It was a Sheep had broke the moorland peace
With his sad cry, a creature who did seem
The blackest thing that ever wore a fleece.

I walked towards him on the stony track
And, pausing for a while between two crags,
I asked him, 'Have you wool upon your back?'
Thus he bespake, 'Enough to fill three bags.'

Most courteously, in measured tones, he told
Who would receive each bag and where they dwelt;
And oft, now years have passed and I am old,
I recollect with joy that inky pelt.

A Nursery Rhyme

as it might have been written by T. S. Eliot

Because time will not run backwards
Because time
Because time will not run
                    Hickory dickory

In the last minute of the first hour
I saw the mouse ascend the ancient timepiece,
Claws whispering like wind in dry hyacinths.

One o'clock,
The street lamp said,
'Remark the mouse that races towards the carpet.'

And the unstilled wheel still turning
                    Hickory dickory
                    Hickory dickory

dock

Waste Land Limericks

I

In April one seldom feels cheerful;
Dry stones, sun and dust make me fearful;
Clairvoyantes distress me,
Commuters depress me –
Met Stetson and gave him an earful.

II

She sat on a mighty fine chair,
Sparks flew as she tidied her hair;
She asks many questions,
I make few suggestions –
Bad as Albert and Lil – what a pair!

III

The Thames runs, bones rattle, rats creep;
Tiresias fancies a peep –
A typist is laid,
A record is played –
Wei la la. After this it gets deep.

IV

A Phoenician called Phlebas forgot
About birds and his business – the lot,
Which is no surprise,
Since he'd met his demise
And been left in the ocean to rot.

V.

No water. Dry rocks and dry throats,
Then thunder, a shower of quotes
From the Sanskrit and Dante.
Da. Damyata. Shantih.
I hope you'll make sense of the notes.

Triolet

I used to think all poets were Byronic –
Mad, bad and dangerous to know.
And then I met a few. Yes it's ironic –
I used to think all poets were Byronic.
They're mostly wicked as a ginless tonic
And wild as pension plans. Not long ago
I used to think all poets were Byronic –
Mad, bad and dangerous to know.

Emily Dickinson

Higgledy-piggledy
Emily Dickinson
Liked to use dashes
Instead of full stops.

Nowadays, faced with such
Idiosyncrasy,
Critics and editors
Send for the cops.

Proverbial Ballade

Fine words won't turn the icing pink;
A wild rose has no employees;
Who boils his socks will make them shrink;
Who catches cold is sure to sneeze.
Who has two legs must wash two knees;
Who breaks the egg will find the yolk;
Who locks his door will need his keys –
So say I and so say the folk.

You can't shave with a tiddlywink,
Nor make red wine from garden peas,
Nor show a blindworm how to blink,
Nor teach an old racoon Chinese.
The juiciest orange feels the squeeze;
Who spends his portion will be broke;
Who has no milk can make no cheese –
So say I and so say the folk.

He makes no blot who has no ink,
Nor gathers honey who keeps no bees.
The ship that does not float will sink;
Who'd travel far must cross the seas.
Lone wolves are seldom seen in threes;
A conker ne'er becomes an oak;
Rome wasn't built by chimpanzees –
So say I and so say the folk.

ENVOI

Dear friends! If adages like these
Should seem banal, or just a joke,
Remember fish don't grow on trees –
So say I and so say the folk.

Advertisement

The lady takes *The Times* and *Vogue*,
Wears Dior dresses, Gucci shoes,
Puts fresh-cut flowers round her room
And lots of carrots in her stews.

A moss-green Volvo, morning walks,
And holidays in Guadeloupe;
Long winter evenings by the fire
With Proust and cream of carrot soup.

Raw carrots on a summer lawn,
Champagne, a Gioconda smile;
Glazed carrots in a silver dish
For Sunday lunch. They call it style.

Lonely Hearts

Can someone make my simple wish come true?
Male biker seeks female for touring fun.
Do you live in North London? Is it you?

Gay vegetarian whose friends are few,
I'm into music, Shakespeare and the sun.
Can someone make my simple wish come true?

Executive in search of something new –
Perhaps bisexual woman, arty, young.
Do you live in North London? Is it you?

Successful, straight and solvent? I am too –
Attractive Jewish lady with a son.
Can someone make my simple wish come true?

I'm Libran, inexperienced and blue –
Need slim non-smoker, under twenty-one.
Do you live in North London? Is it you?

Please write (with photo) to Box 152.
Who knows where it may lead once we've begun?
Can someone make my simple wish come true?
Do you live in North London? Is it you?

On Finding an Old Photograph

Yalding, 1912. My father
in an apple orchard, sunlight
patching his stylish bags;

three women dressed in soft,
white blouses, skirts that brush the grass;
a child with curly hair.

If they were strangers
it would calm me – half-drugged
by the atmosphere – but it does more –

eases a burden
made of all his sadness
and the things I didn't give him.

There he is, happy, and I am unborn.

Tich Miller

Tich Miller wore glasses
with elastoplast-pink frames
and had one foot three sizes larger than the other.

When they picked teams for outdoor games
she and I were always the last two
left standing by the wire-mesh fence.

We avoided one another's eyes,
stooping, perhaps, to re-tie a shoelace,
or affecting interest in the flight

of some fortunate bird, and pretended
not to hear the urgent conference:
'Have Tubby!' 'No, no, have Tich!'

Usually they chose me, the lesser dud,
and she lolloped, unselected,
to the back of the other team.

At eleven we went to different schools.
In time I learned to get my own back,
sneering at hockey-players who couldn't spell.

Tich died when she was twelve.

At 3 a.m.

the room contains no sound
except the ticking of the clock
which has begun to panic
like an insect, trapped
in an enormous box.

Books lie open on the carpet.

Somewhere else
you're sleeping
and beside you there's a woman
who is crying quietly
so you won't wake.

From June to December

1 PRELUDE

It wouldn't be a good idea
To let him stay.
When they knew each other better –
Not today.
But she put on her new black knickers
Anyway.

2 A SERIOUS PERSON

It's nice to meet serious people
And hear them explain their views:
Your concern for the rights of women
Is especially welcome news.

I'm sure you'd never exploit one;
I expect you'd rather be dead;
I'm thoroughly convinced of it –
Now can we go to bed?

3 SUMMER VILLANELLE

You know exactly what to do –
Your kiss, your fingers on my thigh –
I think of little else but you.

It's bliss to have a lover who,
Touching one shoulder, makes me sigh –
You know exactly what to do.

You make me happy through and through,
The way the sun lights up the sky –
I think of little else but you.

I hardly sleep – an hour or two;
I can't eat much and this is why –
You know exactly what to do.

The movie in my mind is blue –
As June runs into warm July
I think of little else but you.

But is it love? And is it true?
Who cares? This much I can't deny:
You know exactly what to do;
I think of little else but you.

4   THE READING

In crumpled, bardic corduroy,
The poet took the stage
And read aloud his deathless verse,
Page by deathless page.

I gazed at him as though intent
On every word he said.
From time to time I'd close my eyes
And smile and nod my head.

He may have thought his every phrase
Sent shivers down my spine.
Perhaps I helped encourage him
To read till half past nine.

Don't ask what it was all about –
I haven't got a clue.
I spent a blissful evening, lost
In carnal thoughts of you.

5   SOME PEOPLE

Some people like sex more than others –
You seem to like it a lot.
There's nothing wrong with being innocent
  or high-minded
But I'm glad you're not.

6   GOING TOO FAR

Cuddling the new telephone directory
After I found your name in it
Was going too far.

It's a safe bet you're not hugging a phone book,
Wherever you are.

7   VERSE FOR A BIRTHDAY CARD

Many happy returns and good luck.
When it comes to a present, I'm stuck.
If you weren't far away
On your own special day,
I could give you a really nice glass of lager.

8   LOVE STORY

I thought you'd be a pushover;
I hoped I wouldn't hurt you.

I warned you this was just a fling
And one day I'd desert you.

So kindly in your spectacles,
So solid in your jacket,
So manly in your big white car
That must have cost a packet.

I grew to like you more and more –
I didn't try to hide it.
Fall in love with someone nice? –
I'd hardly ever tried it.

The course of true love didn't run
Quite the way I'd planned it.
You failed to fall in love with me –
I couldn't understand it.

9 SPRING ONIONS

Decapitating the spring onions,
She made this mental note:
You can tell it's love, the real thing,
When you dream of slitting his throat.

10 I'LL BE NICE

I'll be nice to you and smile –
It's easy for a man to win –
But I'll hate you all the while.

I shall go the extra mile
And condone your every sin –
I'll be nice to you and smile.

You will think I like your style;
You'll believe I've given in
But I'll hate you all the while.

Safe as an atomic pile,
Good as nitroglycerine,
I'll be nice to you and smile.

I'll say hypocrisy is vile
And give a reassuring grin
But I'll hate you all the while.

Set against my wits and guile,
Manly strength won't save your skin.
I'll be nice to you and smile
But I'll hate you all the while.

My Lover

in memory of Robert Gretton 1935–2014

For I will consider my lover, who shall remain nameless.
For at the age of 49 he can make the noise of five different
    kinds of lorry changing gear on a hill.
For he sometimes does this on the stairs at his place of work.
For he is embarrassed when people overhear him.
For he can also imitate at least three different kinds of train.
For these include the London tube train, the steam engine,
    and the Southern Rail electric.
For he supports Tottenham Hotspur with joyful and
    unswerving devotion.
For he abhors Arsenal, whose supporters are uncivilised and
    rough.
For he explains that Spurs are magic, whereas Arsenal are
    boring and defensive.
For I knew nothing of this six months ago, nor did I want to.
For now it all enchants me.
For this he performs in ten degrees.
For first he presents himself as a nice, serious, liberated
    person.
For secondly he sits through many lunches, discussing life
    and love and never mentioning football.
For thirdly he is careful not to reveal how much he dislikes
    losing an argument.
For fourthly he talks about the women in his past,
    acknowledging that some of it must have been his fault.
For fifthly he is so obviously reasonable that you are inclined
    to doubt this.
For sixthly he invites himself round for a drink one evening.
For seventhly you consume two bottles of wine between you.
For eighthly he stays the night.

For ninthly you cannot wait to see him again.
For tenthly this does not happen for several days.
For having achieved his object he turns again to his other interests.
For he will not miss his evening class or his choir practice for a woman.
For he is out nearly all the time.
For you cannot even get him on the telephone.
For he is the kind of man who has been driving women round the bend for generations.
For, sad to say, this thought does not bring you to your senses.
For he is charming.
For he is good with animals and children. For his voice is both reassuring and sexy.
For he drives an A-registration Vauxhall Astra estate. For he goes at 80 miles per hour on the motorways.
For when I plead with him he says, 'I'm not going any slower than *this*.'
For he is convinced he knows his way around better than anyone else on earth.
For he does not encourage suggestions from his passengers.
For if he ever got lost there would be hell to pay.
For he sometimes makes me sleep on the wrong side of my own bed.
For he cannot be bossed around.
For he has this grace, that he is happy to eat fish fingers or Chinese takeaway or to cook the supper himself.
For he knows about my cooking and is realistic.
For he makes me smooth cocoa with bubbles on the top.
For he drinks and smokes at least as much as I do.
For he is obsessed with sex.
For he would never say it is overrated.
For he grew up before the permissive society and remembers his adolescence.

For he does not insist it is healthy and natural, nor does he ask me what I would like him to do.
For he has a few ideas of his own.
For he has never been able to sleep much and talks with me late into the night.
For we wear each other out with our wakefulness.
For he makes me feel like a light-bulb that cannot switch itself off.
For he inspires poem after poem.
For he is clean and tidy but not too concerned with his appearance.
For he lets the barber cut his hair too short and goes round looking like a convict for a fortnight.
For when I ask if this necklace is all right he replies, 'Yes, if no means looking at three others.'
For he was shocked when younger team-mates began using talcum powder in the changing-room.
For his old-fashioned masculinity is the cause of continual merriment on my part.
For this puzzles him.

Rondeau Redoublé

There are so many kinds of awful men –
One can't avoid them all. She often said
She'd never make the same mistake again:
She always made a new mistake instead.

The chinless type who made her feel ill-bred;
The practised charmer, less than charming when
He talked about the wife and kids and fled –
There are so many kinds of awful men.

The half-crazed hippy, deeply into Zen,
Whose cryptic homilies she came to dread;
The fervent youth who worshipped Tony Benn –
'One can't avoid them all,' she often said.

The ageing banker, rich and overfed,
Who held forth on the dollar and the yen –
Though there were many more mistakes ahead,
She'd never make the same mistake again.

The budding poet, scribbling in his den
Odes not to her but to his pussy, Fred;
The drunk who fell asleep at nine or ten –
She always made a new mistake instead.

And so the gambler was at least unwed
And didn't preach or sneer or wield a pen
Or hoard his wealth or take the Scotch to bed.
She'd lived and learned and lived and learned but then
There are so many kinds.

Message

Pick up the phone before it is too late
And dial my number. There's no time to spare –
Love is already turning into hate
And very soon I'll start to look elsewhere.

Good, old-fashioned men like you are rare –
You want to get to know me at a rate
That's guaranteed to drive me to despair.
Pick up the phone before it is too late.

Well, wouldn't it be nice to consummate
Our friendship while we've still got teeth and hair?
Just bear in mind that you are forty-eight
And dial my number. There's no time to spare.

Another kamikaze love affair?
No chance. This time I'll have to learn to wait
But one more day is more than I can bear –
Love is already turning into hate.

Of course, my friends say I exaggerate
And dramatise a lot. That may be fair
But it is no fun being in this state
And very soon I'll start to look elsewhere.

I know you like me but I wouldn't dare
Ring you again. Instead I'll concentrate
On sending thought-waves through the London air
And, if they reach you, please don't hesitate –
Pick up the phone.

Giving Up Smoking

There's not a Shakespeare sonnet
Or a Beethoven quartet
That's easier to like than you
Or harder to forget.

You think that sounds extravagant?
I haven't finished yet –
I like you more than I would like
To have a cigarette.

Manifesto

I'll work, for there's new purpose in my art –
I'll muster all my talent, all my wit
And write the poems that will win your heart.

Pierced by a rusty allegoric dart,
What can I do but make the best of it?
I'll work, for there's new purpose in my art.

You're always on my mind when we're apart –
I can't afford to daydream, so I'll sit
And write the poems that will win your heart.

I am no beauty but I'm pretty smart
And I intend to be your favourite –
I'll work, for there's new purpose in my art.

And if some bloodless literary fart
Says that it's all too personal, I'll spit
And write the poems that will win your heart.

I feel terrific now I've made a start –
I'll have another book before I quit.
I'll work, for there's new purpose in my art,
And write the poems that will win your heart.

II

Mr Strugnell

'This was Mr Strugnell's room,' she'll say,
And look down at the lumpy, single bed.
'He stayed here up until he went away
And kept his bicycle out in that shed.

'He had a job at Norwood library –
He was a quiet sort who liked to read –
Dick Francis mostly, and some poetry –
He liked John Betjeman very much indeed

'But not Pam Ayres or even Patience Strong –
He'd change the subject if I mentioned them,
Or say "It's time for me to run along –
Your taste's too highbrow for me, Mrs M."

'And up he'd go and listen to that jazz.
I don't mind telling you it was a bore –
Few things in this house have been tiresome as
The sound of his foot tapping on the floor.

'He didn't seem the sort for being free
With girls or going out and having fun.
He had a funny turn in 'sixty-three
And ran round shouting "Yippee! It's begun."

'I don't know what he meant but after that
He had a different look, much more relaxed.
Some nights he'd come in late, too tired to chat,
As if he had been somewhat overtaxed.

'And now he's gone. He said he found Tulse Hill
Too stimulating – wanted somewhere dull.
At last he's found a place that fits the bill –
Enjoying perfect boredom up in Hull.'

Budgie Finds His Voice

from The Life and Songs of the Budgie *by Jake Strugnell*

God decided he was tired
Of his spinning toys.
They wobbled and grew still.

When the sun was lifted away
Like an orange lifted from a fruit bowl

And darkness, blacker
Than an oil-slick,
Covered everything forever

And the last ear left on earth
Lay on the beach
Deaf as a shell

And the land froze
And the seas froze

'Who's a pretty boy then?' Budgie cried.

Usquebaugh

Deft, practised, eager,
Your fingers twist the metal cap.
Late into the moth-infested night
We listen to soft scrapings
Of bottle-top on ridged glass,

The plash and glug of amber liquid
Streaming into tumblers, inches deep.
Life-water. Fire-tanged
Hard stuff. Gallons of it,
Sipped and swigged and swallowed.

Whiskey: its terse vowels belie
The slow fuddling and mellowing,
Our guttural speech slurring
Unto warm, thick blather,
The pie-eyed, slug-witted slump

Into soused oblivion –
And the awakening. I long
For pure, cold water as the pump
Creaks in the yard. A bucket
Clatters to the ground. Is agony.

The Lavatory Attendant

*'I counted two and seventy stenches
All well defined and several stinks!'*
— COLERIDGE

Slumped on a chair, his body is an S
That wants to be a minus sign.

His face is overripe Wensleydale
Going blue at the edges.

In overalls of sacerdotal white
He guards a row of fonts

With lids like eye-patches. Snapped shut
They are castanets. All day he hears

Short-lived Niagaras, the clank
And gurgle of canescent cisterns.

When evening comes he sluices a thin tide
Across sand-coloured lino,

Turns Medusa on her head
And wipes the floor with her.

E Pericoloso Sporgersi

But a modulation to D flat minor
argues for pronouns of a different kind:
the consideration of history as syntax
or a slow dance of nomadic stones.
No wonder the flight of the pigeon
over the Piazza Cortina at sunset
becomes a gesture of the purest angst.

Pastruccio knew what to make of such
gratuitous moments, the refractions
of inveterate light. In a garden
of non sequiturs the silkworm dozes,
ignorant of Spinoza and unworried
by sex or the darkening obscurity
of sonorous sentences like these.

My cat piddles on the carpet and yawns.
Art, he reflects, is rivalled only
by a cargo of absolutes sailing northwards
to Goethe's incomparable parakeet.
The gods dream dictionaries and sonatinas.
Beyond the window their shadows lengthen,
aspiring to the stature of a late quartet.

Duffa Rex

I

King of the primeval avenues, the municipal parklands:
architect of the Tulse Hill Poetry Group: life and soul of
the perennial carousals: minstrel: philatelist: long-serving
clerical officer: the friend of everyone who's anyone.
'Pack it in,' said Duffa, 'and buy me a drink.'

II

He digs for the salt-screw, buried in crepitant spud-slivers.
Speaks of his boyhood in the gruntler's yarg, the
unworked cork-bundles, coagulations of nurls.

The mockery of his companions is unabated. It is the
king's round, they urge. His hoard is overripe for
commerce.

One by one he draws coins to the light; examines them:
exemplary silver, his rune stones. Treasure accrued in a
sparse week, to be invested in precious liquid.

Strugnell in Liverpool

for Allen Ginsberg, Charlie Parker,
T. S. Eliot, Paul McCartney, Marcel
Proust and all the other great men
who have influenced my writing

waking early
listening to
birdsong watching
the curtains brighten
like a shirt
washed in Omo
feeling the empty
space beside me
thinking of you

crawling out of
bed searching
for my glasses
piles of clothing
on the carpet
none of it yours

alone in the toilet
with the Harpic
and the Andrex
thinking of you
eating my cornflakes
plastic flowers on
the windowsill green
formica table lovesong

on the radio bacteria
in the drainpipe
thinking of you

going
up
stairs
again
and
getting
dressed

think
ing
of
you

thinking
of you your pink
nylon panties
and your blue
nylon bra
Body Mist
hairsmell of Silvikrin
shampoo and your white
nylon panties

thinking of you

Narrative

The sky was dark, the garden gnomes were still
When Schopenhauer observed, 'I like them less
Than sausages – in fact they make me ill.'
The vicar nodded once and murmured, 'Yes,
But wouldn't Tacitus have praised the skill
Of all those jugglers on the Leeds express?'
It seemed they had decided not to tell
The governors that Fido wasn't well.

Nijinsky's role in this remains mysterious –
We know he knitted cardigans for both
The Spanish twins and, while he was delirious,
Composed an ode to economic growth –
And yet one wonders if Chagall was serious
About the cigarette or merely loath
To recognise that others took for granted
The yellow birdbath he had always wanted.

God and the Jolly Bored Bog-Mouse

Strugnell's entry for the Arvon/Observer Poetry Competition 1980, judged by Ted Hughes, Philip Larkin, Seamus Heaney and Charles Causley.

God tried to teach Mouse how to sing.
'Piss off! I'm not the sort.'
Mouse squelched away across the bog.
'It's jolly cold,' he thought.

Stone-numb, Mouse watched the ice-bright stars,
Decided they were boring.
Cradled in roots and sodden turf,
Soon he was jolly snoring.

Mouse dreamed a Universe of Blood,
He dreamed a shabby room,
He dreamed a dank hole in the earth,
(Back to the jolly womb).

Mouse tried to vomit up his guts
Then got up for a pee.
A comet pulsed across the sky –
He didn't jolly see.

from Strugnell's Sonnets

for D. M. Thomas

(1)

The expense of spirits is a crying shame,
So is the cost of wine. What bard today
Can live like old Khayyam? It's not the same –
A loaf and Thou and Tesco's Beaujolais.
I had this bird called Sharon, fond of gin –
Could knock back six or seven. At the price
I paid a high wage for each hour of sin
And that was why I only had her twice.
Then there was Tracy, who drank rum and Coke,
So beautiful I didn't mind at first
But love grows colder. Now some other bloke
Is subsidising Tracy and her thirst.
I need a woman, honest and sincere,
Who'll come across on half a pint of beer.

(11)

Not from the stars do I my judgement pluck,
Although I often read my horoscope.
Today *The Standard* promises me luck
With money and with girls. One can but hope.
Astrologers may not know if you'll win
The football pools or when you'll get a screw,
But one thing's clearer than this glass of gin –
Their character analyses are true.
Cancerians are sympathetic, kind,
Intuitive, creative, sentimental,
Exceptionally shrewd and, you will find,
They make fantastic lovers, warm and gentle.
Amazing, really, that you fail to see
How very well all this applies to me.

(III)

My glass shall not persuade me I'm senescent,
Nor that it's time to curb my virile hunger.
I'm still as randy as an adolescent
And didn't have much fun when I was younger.
Pursuing girls was hopeless with my looks
(I used to pick my spots and make them worse)
So I consoled myself by reading books –
Philosophy, pornography and verse.
For years I poured my unfulfilled desire
Into sad songs – and now, to my delight,
Find women love a bard, however dire,
And overlook my paunch because I write.
One doesn't need much literary skill
To be the Casanova of Tulse Hill.

(IV)

Not only marble, but the plastic toys
From cornflake packets will outlive this rhyme:
I can't immortalise you, love – our joys
Will lie unnoticed in the vault of time.
When Mrs Thatcher has been cast in bronze
And her administration is a page
In some O-level text-book, when the dons
Have analysed the story of our age,
When travel firms sell tours of outer space
And aeroplanes take off without a sound
And Tulse Hill has become a trendy place
And Upper Norwood's on the underground
Your beauty and my name will be forgotten –
My love is true, but all my verse is rotten.

(v)

How like a sprinter you have turned and run
From me, who'd loved you almost half a year.
The world's become a fridge, there is no sun,
I hardly have the stomach for a beer.
And yet I still have my guitar to strum
And books to read and some fantastic grass
That Tony got me. I sit here and hum
The tunes we used to hear in Norwood bars –
'We Are All Slobs', the Muggers' greatest hit –
Do you remember? Once you said to me,
'This is their best since "Education's Shit"',
And I agreed. But I am forty-three
And blew it when I told you I'd much rather
Listen to a jazz band, like your father.

(VI)

Let me not to the marriage of true swine
Admit impediments. With his big car
He's won your heart, and you have punctured mine.
I have no spare; henceforth I'll bear the scar.
Since women are not worth the booze you buy them
I dedicate myself to Higher Things.
If men deride and sneer, I shall defy them
And soar above Tulse Hill on poet's wings –
A brother to the thrush in Brockwell Park,
Whose song, though sometimes drowned by rock guitars,
Outlives their din. One day I'll make my mark,
Although I'm not from Ulster or from Mars,
And when I'm published in some classy mag
You'll rue the day you scarpered in his Jag.

(VII)

'At the moment, if you're seen reading poetry in a train, the carriage empties instantly.'
— ANDREW MOTION in a *Guardian* interview

Indeed 'tis true. I travel here and there
On British Rail a lot. I've often said
That if you haven't got the first-class fare
You really need a book of verse instead.
Then, should you find that all the seats are taken,
Brandish your Edward Thomas, Yeats or Pound.
Your fellow passengers, severely shaken,
Will almost all be loath to stick around.
Recent research in railway sociology
Shows it's best to read the stuff aloud:
A few choice bits from Motion's new anthology
And you'll be lonelier than any cloud.
This stratagem's a godsend to recluses
And demonstrates that poetry has its uses.

from Strugnell's *Rubáiyát*

1

Awake! for Morning on the Pitch of Night
Has whistled and has put the Stars to Flight.
The incandescent football in the East
Has brought the splendour of Tulse Hill to Light.

7

Another Pint! Come, loosen up, have Fun!
Fling off your Hang-Ups and enjoy the Sun:
Time's Spacecraft all too soon will carry you
Away – and Lo! the Countdown has begun.

11

Here with a Bag of Crisps beneath the Bough,
A Can of Beer, a Radio – and Thou
Beside me half-asleep in Brockwell Park
And Brockwell Park is Paradise enow.

12

Some Men to everlasting Bliss aspire,
Their Lives, Auditions for the heavenly Choir:
Oh, use your Credit Card and waive the Rest –
Brave Music of a distant Amplifier!

26

Oh, come with Strugnell – Argument's no Tonic.
One thing's certain: Life flies supersonic.
One thing's certain, Man's Evasion chronic:
The Flower that's blown can never be bionic.

51

The Moving Telex writes and having writ
Moves on; nor all thy Therapy nor Wit
Shall lure it back to cancel half a line
Nor Daz nor Bold wash out a Word of it.

Strugnell's Haiku

(I)

The cherry blossom
In my neighbour's garden – Oh!
It looks really nice.

(II)

The leaves have fallen
And the snow has fallen and
Soon my hair also . . .

(III)

November evening:
The moon is up, rooks settle,
The pubs are open.

Notes on the Parodies in Section II

Page 37: A parody of Philip Larkin.
Page 39: A parody of Ted Hughes.
Page 40: A parody of Seamus Heaney.
Page 41: A parody of Craig Raine.
Page 42: A parody of Peter Porter.
Page 43: A parody of Geoffrey Hill.
Page 44: A parody of Adrian Henri.
Page 46: My editor thought this was a parody of James Fenton. It may have been influenced by him but it is the result of a game called *bouts-rimés*. The rhymes are given and you have to fill in the rest. It was a *New Statesman* or *Spectator* competition.
Page 47: Explained in the epigraph.
Pages 48–54: Strugnell's sonnets are not parodies of Shakespeare, although the first lines are slightly altered versions of his, and they use the Shakespearean sonnet form.

III

III

Making Cocoa for Kingsley Amis

It was a dream I had last week
And some kind of record seemed vital.
I knew it wouldn't be much of a poem
But I love the title.

UNCOLLECTED POEMS

— 1973–1985 —

Depression

You lie, snail-like, on your stomach –
I dare not speak or touch,
Knowing too well the ways of our kind –
The retreat, the narrowing spiral.

We are both convinced it is impossible
To close the distance.
I can no more cross this room
Than Zeno's arrow.

Going Away

On the platform where the school train left,
Seven years old, she didn't cry
But smiled and chattered
Like the schoolgirls she had met in books,
Kissed her parents and went away.
She never really came back.

The dormitory was dark. She longed
For one slim triangle of moonlight
Where the curtains didn't meet.
It was as if black felt
Were pressed against her face
And it was hard to breathe.

And now she hurries through affairs
Like someone with a train to catch –
She knows that every love
Will end in brave farewell –
And, every time, she visits once again
The blackness of that room.

The Journey

The journey was difficult at first
Until I shipped my oars,
Let the river sweep me on,
Lifted my eyes from the dark brown water
And the search for rocks,
Saw the land, the sky, glide past.

My boat will complete the journey.
I do not know where the winding river leads.
I do not ask who will arrive.

Midstream and faithful to the current,
I do not look downwards
As I reach the waterfall.

There is no wind –
Only the power of the water.

Score

Shadows of lamp posts
stretch across the road.

If you could pluck one
it would make a thick, deep sound.

Imagine you are travelling across the strings
of a huge grand piano.

Add to this the way leaf shadows
scrape the tarmac, softly,

and the high notes of the pavement
as it catches points of light.

Begin to hum a slow, free tune
you haven't heard before.

Word-Watching

for Paul McCloud

He has drawn lines
Halfway down the page
And covered them
With half a story.

Now he pauses,
Searching the air.

If he draws another line
And keeps very still,
Perhaps some words
Will come and sit on it.

Thaw

Under trees
the sound is loud, irregular, staccato.

Like aged priests
more used to contemplative prayer

they are baptising us
with stiff and bony hands.

Sunset at Widemouth Bay

Fire
behind the sea.
The sky is full of long-winged angels,
burning.

Grandmother

Grandmother, one tooth,
Chews nuts with the urgency
Of a young squirrel.

Sisters

My sister
was the bad one –
said what she thought
and did what she liked
and didn't care.

At ten she wore
a knife tucked in
her leather belt
dreamed of *being*
a prince on a white horse.

Became a dolly bird
with dyed hair longer
than her skirts, pulling
the best of the local talent.
Mother wept and prayed.

At thirty she's divorced,
has cropped her locks
and squats in Hackney –
tells me 'God created man
then realised Her mistake.'

I'm not like her,
I'm good – but now
I'm working on it.
Fighting through
to my own brand of badness

I am glad of her
at last – her conferences,
her anger, and her boots.
we talk and smoke
and laugh at everybody –

two bad sisters.

My Favourite Game

Loving you is my favourite game,
Combining the pleasures of chess and roulette.
I study the gambits. I place one more bet.

If I'm a fanatic, that smile is to blame –
I've been under a spell since the first time we met.
Loving you is my favourite game.

The odds are against me, I know. All the same,
I'll play up and play up and banish regret
And – who knows? – I could hit a winning streak yet.
Loving you is my favourite game.

Current Affairs

(February 1985)

*in memory of Richard Lindley,
television reporter, 1936–2019*

When will the miners go back underground?
Will Scargill yet contrive to save his face?
Can anything be done about the pound?
Will Nigel Lawson end up in disgrace?
Is Thatcher a disaster or an ace?
Has the electorate been sold a pup?
Will Reagan greet her with a warm embrace?
Will Richard Lindley ever ring me up?

Will Kinnock's accusations all rebound?
Who made decisions in the Ponting case
And will the missing log-book soon be found?
Will Heseltine fence off another base?
How long can old Chernenko stand the pace?
Are Liverpool front-runners for the Cup?
Is there a future for the human race?
Will Richard Lindley ever ring me up?

ENVOI

Sisters! Is love's pursuit a hopeless chase?
Are men bad news? Should I know better? Yup.
Will dreaming make the world a happier place?
Will Richard Lindley ever ring me up?

Revenge

My next project
will be a beautifully produced collection
of poems about photographers.

I shall call it
British Photographers of Our Time
and none of them will want to be left out.

I'll need to visit each one in his home
(or hers) and make notes.
It will take at least three hours.

If I feel at all unhappy
about the arrangement of the furniture or pictures,
I shall expect them to change it.
By the time I leave, the photographer
may well be covered in dust.

I shall take with me a holdall
containing bulky equipment
and I shall spread it all over the living-room floor.
The most important item will be the lights,
which I shall shine on my subjects' faces
to get a better view of their blackheads.

Uncooperative or bad-tempered photographers
will get nasty poems. They know this.
Most of them will be perfectly sweet to me
and give me tea and cakes.

But should I, even so, be moved
to write an unkind poem,
then I must obey my Muse.
They'll understand this –
they are artists too.

And if my book sells,
they'll be laid out on the nation's coffee tables,
warts and all, in large clear print.

I hope they will appreciate the honour.
The royalties, of course,
will all be mine.

from Strugnell's Sonnets

(VIII)

When in disgrace with fortune and the boss,
Too skint to buy a seventh pint of beer,
I've troubled the barmaid with my tale of loss
And snuffled back a stray, unmanly tear,
I stagger home, collapsing on the bed
And wonder how a talent such as mine
Can go unrecognised, my works unread –
Pearls far too subtle for the eyes of swine
Such as the editors who send them back
From *Lemons* or *The Crazy Frog* or *Sludge*.
I sometimes wonder if I shouldn't pack
The whole thing in. But who are they to judge?
Posterity divides true bards from amateurs
And time will be the test of these pentameters.

(IX)

Oh, never say that I was false of tongue,
Though actions seemed my words to qualify.
I told you not long after you first flung
Yourself at me: I can admit no tie.
Free spirit, poet, one who needs a range
Of women to inspire his deathless verse –
It is for Art's sake that I like a change
Of bird from time to time. Don't weep and curse.
I love you, love all women. I'm sincere
And tender, and I write about them well.
Why did the twenty-three I had last year
All end up telling me to go to hell?
'Oh, what do women want?' the sages cry.
I wonder as I bathe my blackened eye.

(X)

How sober was I when I took my way
To read my verses at a pub in Purley.
The evening might have turned out quite OK
Had I not reached the venue far too early.
I thought that I should have a Scotch or two
To calm my nerves and get me in the mood.
Then Tony turned up and we had a few –
By eight o'clock we were completely slewed.
What followed is a blur. I nearly fell
Right off the platform several times, I'm told.
My little jokes did not go down too well,
My *Songs of Upper Norwood* left them cold.
Oh fellow bards, however great your need,
Best stick to orange juice before you read.

(XI)

Shall I compare a summer's day to you
Or not? You know how miserable it gets:
May winds rough up a darling bud or two
And English summers always take short lets.
Sometime "Phew what a scorcher!" we all say
And often is the weather dull and cold;
And everyone goes off a bit some day –
It's either bad luck or they're growing old.
But, thanks to me, your summer is immortal,
Your looks shall be preserved from year to year,
Nor shall Death brag you've wandered through his portal
When anyone who reads can find you here.
While men can breathe you'll live in this my song –
At least, I hope so but I could be wrong.

Strugnell's Bargain

My true love hath my heart and I have hers:
We swapped last Tuesday and felt quite elated
But now, whenever one of us refers
To 'my heart', things get rather complicated.
Just now, when she complained, 'My heart is racing',
'You mean my heart is racing,' I replied.
'That's what I said.' 'You mean the heart replacing
Your heart, my love.' Oh piss off Jake,' she cried.
I ask you, do you think Sir Philip Sidney
Got spoken to like that? And I suspect
If I threw in my liver and a kidney
She'd still address me with as scant respect.
Therefore do I revoke my opening line:
My love can keep her heart and I'll have mine.

A Shorter Version of Wordsworth's Immortality Ode

To a mite
Things look bright.
Later on
Glory gone.
Still must say
I'm OK –
Wise old sort,
Into thought.

Ballad of an Office Romance

He was a middle manager,
Past forty, still quite spry,
And she the pretty young trainee
Who caught his roving eye.

'Oh are you busy after work?
And shall we have a drink?
Don't look so suspicious love –
I'm nicer than you think.'

He took her to a little place.
The wine was cheap and bad
And, after a carafe or two,
They went back to her pad.

'I met my love in Personnel,
I brought him home to bed.
My heart is singing. I can't say
The same about my head.'

They drank their tea and Alka-Seltzer,
Hugged again and sighed.
'I wish you were a bachelor
And I could be a bride.'

'Who cares for rings and licences?
My marriage is a sham.
I could soon be in love with you.
In fact, I think I am.'

Thereafter every Tuesday night,
Sometimes on Thursdays too,
The lovers met at half past six
And did what lovers do.

'I love you, Len, with all my heart;
I'll love you all my life.
But we must kiss and say goodbye
Unless you leave your wife.'

'I'll leave her when the spring is here.
The twins will be eighteen
And I'll be free to come and live
With you in Willesden Green.'

But when the buds of spring appeared
He wasn't in a hurry –
The garden looked so beautiful
Outside his home in Surrey.

'You have not left your home and wife,
You have not left your garden.
The daffodils have withered now
And soon my heart will harden.'

'I'll leave her in the summertime
When groundsmen roll the wicket.
Just two more months. I shan't renew
My current season ticket.'

'The summer flowers have expired,
So has your annual season.
So why do you delay, my love?
Just give me one good reason.'

'I'll leave her when the autumn comes –
I think it would be fairer –
When I have paid the last instalment
On the new Sierra.'

'It's cold November and the shops
Are full of Christmas cheer.
This is our anniversary –
I've loved you for a year.'

'After Christmas, oh my darling,
There'll be no more waiting.
First I have to mend the roof
And do some decorating.'

Reader, he went and lived with her –
It lasted thirteen days.
It can be hard at forty-four
To change one's little ways.

The cooking wasn't up to scratch,
His shirts were folded wrong.
In two rooms with one window-box
The weekend seemed so long.

'A man must do what he must do
And I know what is right.
My conscience will not let me stay.'
He left on Friday night.

He begged forgiveness from his wife
And pulled himself together,
Planning all the things he'd do
Come the warmer weather.

He'd build a swimming-pool and then
A timber-frame extension.
He had a few regrets, of course –
Almost too few to mention.

She spends her weekends all alone,
Dining on beans and bacon.
Who thinks that love will find a way
Is frequently mistaken.

This is uncollected because I was afraid people would assume it was an episode from my own love life. It isn't.

THE RIVER GIRL

— 1991 —

Illustrated by Nicholas Garland

The River Girl is based on a plot outline by Gren Middleton of the Movingstage Marionette Company, who commissioned the poem for performance.

An English meadow, early in the morning.
The Thames has whispered through another night
And now the sun is coming out and touching
The water and the grass with summer light.

The river rises in a shallow valley
And flows across our green and pleasant land
Two hundred miles and more until fresh water
Turns salt, and muddy banks give way to sand.

In Gloucestershire a stream, it meets the ocean
A mighty thoroughfare, deep, wide and strong.
It knew our forebears. It will know our children.
Sweet Thames run softly till I end my song.

And who is this, who sits beside the river
Day after day and gazes at the sky
With searching eyes and gazes at the water
And frowns and shakes his head with many a sigh?

A would-be poet, seeking inspiration.
He has a notebook. Every page is white
And blank. He sits and sits and dreams of greatness.
He dreams of greatness but he cannot write.

And yet the merest glance tells the observer
That here's a man devoted to his art –
Long hair, pale face and crumpled corduroy trousers.
He knows a thing or two. He looks the part.

Beneath the river's smooth and quiet surface,
Where fishes play and water-weeds unfurl
In dappled sunlight, lives the lovely Isis,
Giver of dreams, enchantress, river girl.

As soon as Isis sees the handsome poet,
She breaks the surface. Floating in a dress
Of purest white, she's graceful as a lily
(Where most of us, of course, would look a mess).

The handsome poet sees the lovely Isis
And gasps and cannot take his eyes away.
He smiles. She smiles. It is an old, old story.
Love at first sight. It happens every day.

Oh, love's a powerful, fast-moving current
That seizes us before we've time to think.
And some of us it carries on to safety
Upon a happy shore, while others sink.

And these two? We shall see. She floats towards him
As, silently, he stretches out his hand.
She takes it and he tries to pull her to him.
She shakes her head. He doesn't understand.

'Oh come and walk with me, enchanting maiden.
Climb up this bank. Enjoy the summer weather.
Like young lambs, we will frolic in the meadows.
Oh come, let us be lyrical together.

'Your hair will dry and gleam like finest satin.
I'll gather flowers and make a little crown
And place it on your head and call you "Princess" –
Good heavens. Hang on. I must write this down.'

He lets her go and scribbles in his notebook.
A miracle! He is in love and *writing*.
When he looks up and smiles, his eyes are blazing –
'My love. My Muse. Oh, this is so exciting.'

She smiles as well. And, since she has a secret,
She looks a little bit like La Gioconda,
Which does no harm at all. His heart turns over.
With every passing second he grows fonder.

'My love is like a young and tender sapling.
My love is like a rose without a thorn.
Coming to banish misery and darkness,
My love is like the first light of the dawn.

'These words! Where are they coming from, my darling?'
She knows, says nothing, looks down at the river.
For if he guesses, or if she should tell him,
So much the worse for her. Fear makes her shiver.

'You're cold, my love. Please come and sit beside me.
I want to keep you warm and safe and never
Let go of you. You're beautiful. You're magic.
Come here, come now, and stay with me for ever.

'Your eyes are saying yes, though you are silent.'
He grasps her hand again. He grasps her shoulder
And kisses her, and kissing gives such pleasure,
He cannot help but grow a little bolder.

She breaks away. 'My love, I have to go now.
Be here tomorrow and we'll meet again.
The night will seem too long. I'll count the minutes
And think about you all the time till then.'

'Don't go. Don't go. I beg you, do not leave me
Alone, to suffer passionate distress.
Look, are you on the phone? Give me your number.'
'There's no phone where I'm going.' 'Your address?'

But as he speaks, she's vanished underwater
And, surfacing a hundred yards downstream,
She calls to him. 'My darling. Do not follow.
We'll meet tomorrow. Now go home and dream.'

'Go home and dream.' He turns away and murmurs
Like one bewitched, and walks towards the town.
'Go home and dream.' He is already dreaming
Of kisses and . . . No. Best not write it down –

This is for families. Let's say he's happy.
He is in love, he's lost, on fire, possessed.
We'll leave him wandering dreamily to Oxford,
His notebook clasped to his impassioned breast.

We'll leave the world we know and follow Isis
Into her world, the kingdom underwater
That's ruled by Father Thames. And she must find him –
Our heroine is Father Thames's daughter,

Adopted by him when she was a baby
But that was many centuries ago.
You wonder who she is and where she came from
And why? Ask Father Thames. I do not know.

But I can tell you that he loves her dearly –
Though he can be forbidding, angry, cold,
He loves his daughter. She's his joy, his treasure.
He'd like to keep her with him, now he's old.

But he is wise, too wise to think a daughter
Can be contented with a father's love.
He dreads the day some other love will beckon
And call his Isis to the world above.

'Where are you, Father?' He can hear her calling –
A distant cry at first, then it comes near.
'O Father! Father!' – breathless and excited –
He stands up tall. He will not show his fear.

He stands up tall and welcomes her. 'My daughter!'
She looks at him and sees his face is stern.
She hesitates. Will he be understanding
Or spoil it all with fatherly concern?

Oh why is he so strict and so old-fashioned?
She is afraid to speak, now she has found him.
She'd better kneel and take his hand and kiss it –
Such gestures often help her get around him.

And when she's kissed his hand, she gazes at him
Most solemnly. She's wide-eyed with respect.
And when his aged face begins to soften,
She knows all this is having some effect.

'Arise, my daughter. We will sit together –
I am an old man and I need to rest.
And you can tell me why you're so excited,
Although I think I have already guessed.'

'Father, I met a man.' He nods. 'Continue.'
'He is the one for me. I'm sure, I know it.
If you could see his face! He's good. He's noble
And handsome. Father, this man is a poet!'

Her father sighs. It's worse than he expected.
To lose her to a man at all is bad
But to a poet! He has seen these poets
In action. 'Father, you look very sad.

'Dear Father, I have never disobeyed you.
I love you and remember what you said –
That I must never, never leave the river –
And when he asked me to, I shook my head.

'But now I have to ask you for my freedom
To come and go.' She's trying not to cry.
'I promise that I'll come and see you often
But if I'm not with him, I think I'll die.'

'My child, my child, now calm yourself and listen.
I am too old to think that anyone
Can argue with a young girl's love. A parent
May just as well attempt to quench the sun.

'If you have lost your heart, I can't retrieve it,
So I will let you go, yes, with my blessing.
But first I have a gift for you, to help you
To fascinate this poet and keep him guessing.

'The magic powers you possess already
Enable you, dear child, to be a giver
Of words and dreams. Today I will enhance them
Before you leave me and our lovely river.'

He stands. 'Now, Isis, come and stand before me.'
He grasps her head and holds it very tight,
Closes his eyes, and, fierce with concentration,
He speaks so loudly that the fish take fright.

'You powers that rule the rivers and the oceans,
You powers from whom my magic power stems,
Now manifest yourselves in these quiet waters.
I summon you to help me, Father Thames.'

And suddenly the water all around them
Grows turbulent. 'Spirits, now you are here
I ask you to confer the gift of changing
Upon this river girl, my child so dear.

'Give her the power to transform her body
Into the shape of any living thing –
Of furry beast, or bird or fish or flower,
So she may hide, be fierce, run fast, take wing.'

He moves away from Isis, leaves her standing
Alone. The turbulence intensifies.
It closes round her and becomes a vortex.
'I want . . . I want to be a fish!' she cries.

No sooner said than done. Now she is breathing
Through gills. She flaps her fins and tail with grace.
The water's calm again. She swims to Father
And plants a fishy kiss upon his face,

Then swims away and hides behind a boulder
And, when she reappears, she is herself.
She laughs, delighted with her own performance.
Her father smiles. She's still his little elf.

But when he speaks, he's serious and solemn.
'If this man marries you, he will grow strong.
Now go and find him. Go and find your poet.
Come back and visit me before too long.'

He holds her to his breast, then turns abruptly
And strides away, upright, his head held high.
And Isis suddenly feels very lonely
And sad. 'Goodbye, Old Father Thames, goodbye.'

At last she turns away and swims downriver,
Leaving her happy childhood world behind
And looking forward to a happy future.
Good luck, sweet maiden, and may life be kind.

Six months have passed. Our lovers now are married,
Living together in a little flat.
He writes and writes. She is his Muse and soulmate.
The cooking and the housework? She does that.

And she is happy just to be beside him
And when her lovely eyes meet his, they shine.
And every time he looks upon his darling,
He dreams up yet another telling line.

It's wonderful. His writer's block has melted –
Since he met her, he's had so much to say
That he has filled up notebook after notebook
And words are dancing in his head all day.

And words are singing of the world around him –
How beautiful it is, for now he sees
With lover's eyes, and everything is altered.
He's come alive. He's growing like the trees.

He's opening like flowers in the sunshine,
He's flowing like the river, sure and strong,
And, what is more, some people think it likely
That he will be in print before too long.

Last month he sent his work to Tite and Snobbo,
The publishers. Now he must wait and wonder
If it will go down well with that famed poet,
Tite's editor, the dreaded Clinton Thunder.

He knows it's good but will Clint Thunder like it?
Or will he have to try the Hatchet Press
Up North, or even Doolittle and Dalley?
And what if nobody at all says yes?

'A cup of tea, my love?' 'Oh, Isis, thank you.
Just what I wanted. Has the postman been?'
'Not yet. He's late.' 'He's late and you are lovely.
I want to kiss you, darling wife, my queen.'

Yes, they are happy. Long may they remain so.
He hears a noise and looks up. 'What was that?'
'The post?' 'Now keep your fingers crossed, my angel.'
He runs to see what's landed on the mat.

'It's here! It's here! This is from Tite and Snobbo!'
Opening it, he shakes with hope and fear.
'Yes, it's from Thunder. And he likes my poems
And says they want to publish me next year!

'Yoo hoo! Yoo hoo!' He's jumping on the armchairs,
He's dancing round the room. 'Come and be kissed,
My Muse, my love, my life, my inspiration,
Your husband's on the Tite and Snobbo list!'

Isis is overwhelmed. He finds a hanky
And wipes the tears from her beloved face,
And strokes her hair and puts his arms around her
And holds her in a long, long, long embrace.

The planet Earth has made another journey
Around the sun, the seasons came and went,
Things grew and died. In due course Tite and Snobbo
Produced the book. A publishing event!

The critics loved it and the public bought it
And it won three awards. Of course, such glory
Is very rarely won by any poet –
Remember that this is a fairy story.

And there is something that the storyteller
Forgot to mention. It's the hero's name:
He's called John Didde. That's D–I–D–D–E, yes,
A little like John Donne, of greater fame.

But now John Didde, too, is a name to conjure
At dinner, if you're up to date and arty.
And he is in demand. Young John and Isis
Spend every other evening at some party,

Where he is lionised by men and women:
'John Didde! Congratulations! Lovely book!'
'John Didde! I have been desperate to meet you.
I, too, write poems. Would you take a look?'

'Excuse me. I must have a word with John here.
Some time soon, could I do an interview?'
'Of course. Now here's my wife. I'll introduce you.'
She looks at Isis coldly. 'How do you do?'

Poor Isis wanders off into a corner.
She's trying not to sulk but she'd prefer
To be at home, away from all these people,
Though, even there, things aren't quite what they were.

He's made a lot of new friends, mostly poets,
Who visit him and talk for hours on end
About who's good, who's second-rate, who's dreadful.
I feel for her. It drives me round the bend

And I'm supposed to *be* a poet. Sometimes
They're rude enough to make poor Isis weep.
Her husband drinks an awful lot of whisky
And, when the last one leaves, he falls asleep.

He's lively now. He's talking to that woman.
Look at her face, at those seductive eyes.
'No, jealousy is ugly. I'm above it.
I'm Isis of the River Thames.' She sighs.

'I'm Isis of the River Thames. O Father,
In all this time I've only seen you twice.
There was so much to do. Time passed so quickly.
You might have given me some good advice.

'I've left it far too long. I'll come tomorrow
To your cool, quiet river-world and tell
My sorrows, with my head upon your shoulder,
And ask you what to do, and listen well.'

Down, down into the half-light of the river,
Isis dives. The water strokes her limbs
And she remembers how she loves to be here.
She turns a somersault and swims and swims,

As lithe as any fish. And all the creatures
Who see her pass are happy that she's here.
The bolder fishes nuzzle her in friendship
And one forgets himself and bites her ear.

'Ouch! Stop it! I am looking for my father.
Do you know where he is?' They swim ahead,
Her pilots, to the underwater bower
Where he lies sleeping on the riverbed.

He's sleeping soundly, and he looks so peaceful
She doesn't like to wake him. She prefers
To sit beside him and enjoy the water
And listen to its music, till he stirs.

'Isis, my darling girl. Am I still dreaming?
Give me your hand. I think it's really you.
At last you've come to see your poor old father
And brought that smile of yours. Ah yes. It's true.

'And how's your poet? Loving, kind and faithful?
Treating his lovely wife the way he should?
Behaving better than the other poets?'
'The truth is, Father, things are not too good.

'He's doing well. He has become quite famous
And lots of people want to know him now.
He's not the same. I feel as if I've lost him.
I want to win him back. I don't know how.'

'Oh this is sad but it does not surprise me.'
His arm's around her. They sit side by side.
'Pity the woman with a human husband.
Pity most of all the poet's bride.'

'He's very insecure.' 'I do not doubt it.'
'I think that if he lost me, he'd be sad,
But nowadays he flirts with other women
And drinks too much.' 'Isis, all poets are mad.

'Do you still love him?' 'Yes, I love him, Father.'
'Then listen carefully to my advice.
This poet owes a lot to you and sometimes
Those who give too freely pay a price.

'There is wisdom in the human saying:
"It's easier to give than to receive."
He knows you are his Muse and inspiration
And wonders what will happen, if you leave.

'And no man wants to feel he is dependent
Upon his wife. Sometimes, perhaps, he thinks
It's all too easy. He can't understand it.
He turns his back on you. He flirts. He drinks.

'From now on, Isis, be a little sparing
And cunning in the way you use your powers.
Clever Muses sometimes leave their poets
Suffering despair for hours and hours

'Or days or weeks or months.' 'Oh, that is cruel!'
'It is. Perhaps a day or two's enough.
My daughter, you are generous and loving.
Your father should have taught you to be tough.

'Do not forget the wedding-gift I gave you.
It may be useful in your hour of need.
But never let him know you have the power
To change yourself. He must not know. Take heed.'

'Father, I knew you'd help. I kneel and thank you.
Things will be better now. I'm sure.' 'We'll see.
Go live a little longer with your husband
And, if it doesn't work, come back to me.'

John Didde at home with literary cronies,
All well away on whisky, wine and beer.
And where is Isis? She is in the kitchen.
No one will notice that she isn't here.

'You're telling me, John – are you? – quite sincerely,
You think Clint Thunder's *good*? I disagree,'
Says one, in drunken tones. 'I hate the bastard.
If he knew anything, he'd publish *me*.

'Ha. Ha.' He laughs a drunken laugh and staggers
Out to another room. He's feeling ill.
'What are you working on, John?' asks a woman.
'Not much. Not much. Some days the output's nil.'

'But everybody says you're so prolific.'
'I was. But now, it seems, I'm slowing down.'
'Too many lunches?' Look, her eyes are twinkling.
'Perhaps. Too many journeys up to town.'

They smile at one another very fondly.
The others watch. Is something going on?
Suddenly a cat runs from the kitchen,
Miaowing. Jumping up, it lands on John.

'This wretched cat. I don't know where it comes from.'
He picks it up and puts it on the floor.
It leaps again and curls up on the woman.
'Ah, Moggy. What a nice puss. Shake a paw.'

The cat snarls nastily. Its claws look vicious.
Is it going to scratch the lady's face?
The lady squeals and John comes to the rescue.
'Cat. Out of here. Get out. You're in disgrace.'

They get back to their literary chatter.
The kitchen door is opening, just a crack,
While through the other door a body slouches –
A very drunken poet, coming back.

Slowly, slowly making for the sofa.
Another step or two and he'll be there.
A dark shape streaks across the room and trips him.
He's on the sofa, bottom in the air.

Oh what a sound! What fearsome, dreadful groaning!
The others pick him up and sit him down.
'Who tripped me, John?' 'It was that cat, the beggar.'
'The cat,' he echoes, with a drunken frown.

'That cat,' says John. 'It looks as if it's laughing.
Look at it. It's not sorry. No, it's glad!'
'Is it a he or she?' inquires another,
'And what's its name?' 'Don't know. I call it BAD!'

Poor cat. She slinks away into the kitchen.
Am I quite sure the cat's a she? Oh, yes.
She's got it wrong. She wanted some attention
And went too far with all this naughtiness.

'Time to be off.' 'Me too. I must be going.'
'Where's Isis, John? We ought to say goodbye.'
'It doesn't matter. I expect she's sleeping.'
'She doesn't want to talk to us.' 'She's shy.'

'Well, thanks a lot. It was a lovely evening.'
John goes along and sees them down the stairs,
And Isis reappears, out of the kitchen.
She tidies things away and pats the chairs.

'I thought you were in bed.' 'No, in the kitchen.'
'I see. You know that wretched cat got in.
You must have seen it.' Isis doesn't answer.
She cannot lie. She gives a little grin.

'I'm turning in. I'm tired. Goodnight, darling.'
'John.' 'What?' 'It doesn't matter. Go and sleep.
I won't be long.' She sits down, crying – softly,
For no man likes to hear a woman weep,

Especially if he's the cause. But, Isis,
You must not cry all night. You need some rest.
Perhaps things will be better in the morning.
Perhaps all this will turn out for the best.

Perhaps not. But we have to manage somehow.
We tell ourselves, to keep despair away,
That things can seem much better in the morning
And that tomorrow is another day.

Tomorrow never comes. Today's beginning
And John is up. He's packed a little bag.
'Are you going somewhere?' Isis asks him.
'I need to go to London. It's a drag.

'I'll be a day or two.' 'You didn't tell me.'
'I have to go. Now please don't make a scene.
You'll be all right and I'll be back by Friday.
I'll tell you what I've done and where I've been.'

He leaves the room. His wife, at last, is angry,
Too angry to be sensible, and that
Is why she calls once more upon the spirits:
'Change me! Change me! I want to be a cat!'

When John comes back, there is no sign of Isis,
Just this fierce, snarling animal. 'Oh no!
I've had enough. This time, cat, it's the basket.'
He fetches it and grabs her. 'In you go.'

'Miaow! Miaow!' John finds a pen and paper.
'Isis, where are you? Got to go. Please try
To find a good home for this noisy creature,
As far away as possible. Goodbye.'

He rushes out and slams the door behind him.
'Miaow! Miaow!' What can poor Isis do?
Her body's far too big for this small basket.
She can't change back. She gives a piteous mew

And then falls silent. There's no one to feed her.
She's trapped. But look. Can you see what I see?
Old Father Thames! Is this a dream? A vision?
'If it doesn't work, come back to me.

'Come back to me. Come back to me, my daughter.'
He disappears without another word
And Isis acts. This monstrous caterwauling
Means something. 'Spirits! Come! Make me a bird!'

The caterwauling stops. Now she is hopping
Around the basket. 'Tap, tap', go her feet.
Yes, Isis is a bird. She is a swallow.
Her feathers shine. And she can sing. 'T-weet.'

And now it's easy to escape. She squeezes
Her avian body through a narrow hole.
She looks around her. Everything's enormous.
She shakes herself and takes a little stroll,

Then flaps her wings a bit and soon she's flying,
Soaring, swooping, landing on the floor,
And hovering, at last, before John's photo.
She gazes. She won't see him anymore.

For she is leaving. Yes, she has decided.
Sad, that this is how it has to be.
She turns and flies towards an open window
And out into the sky. She's gone. She's free.

Over gardens, over streets and rooftops,
Past dreaming spires and towers, Isis flies.
Our enchanting princess of the river
Has become a princess of the skies.

Over woods and ponds and hills and meadows
Until she comes at last to that same place
Where once there sat a young and handsome poet
With an unhappy frown upon his face.

Gracefully the swallow skims the river,
Then, landing on a bough, she rests her wings.
'T-weet. T-weet.' She's calling to the spirits.
'T-weet. I want to be myself,' she sings.

Isis of the River Thames is standing
Upon the river bank, her head held high,
Older and wiser than the simple maiden
Who gave her heart away. Now, say goodbye –

For Isis won't be back, not in our lifetime.
One day, perhaps, when several hundred years
Have healed the wound, she'll meet our children's children
Beside the Thames. She dives and disappears.

Now who is this who walks beside the river
Day after day, and gazes at the sky
With searching eyes and gazes at the water
And weeps and shakes his head with many a sigh?

Ah John, poor John. When he got back from London,
He looked for Isis. He looked everywhere.
Weeks, months have passed and still he goes on hoping
That one day he'll come home and find her there

And take her in his arms and say he loves her.
Tormented by self-hatred and regret,
He haunts the places where they went together
And most of all this place, where first they met.

The sky is weeping too. The water's rising.
It is as if the Thames cannot contain
Such grief. The river's high and overflowing
Until the fields are lakes of tears and rain.

When they tell the story of this summer,
You'll hear about the weather and the flood
And how the River Thames at last retreated
And how the sun came out and dried the mud

And life went on. Poor John will manage somehow
And one day, maybe, you will chance to find
A copy of his book. Within its pages,
Isis still enchants the human mind.

Now they sleep, and hidden hands are resting.
It's almost time for you to go, dear friends.
A swallow sings. The sun sets on the river.
Sweet Thames run softly as our story ends.

SERIOUS CONCERNS

— 1992 —

Flowers

Some men never think of it.
You did. You'd come along
And say you'd nearly brought me flowers
But something had gone wrong.

The shop was closed. Or you had doubts –
The sort that minds like ours
Dream up incessantly. You thought
I might not want your flowers.

It made me smile and hug you then.
Now I can only smile.
But, look, the flowers you nearly brought
Have lasted all this while.

Defining the Problem

I can't forgive you. Even if I could,
You wouldn't pardon me for seeing through you.
And yet I cannot cure myself of love
For what I thought you were before I knew you.

The Aerial

The aerial on this radio broke
A long, long time ago,
When you were just a name to me –
Someone I didn't know.

The man before the man before
Had not yet set his cap
The day a clumsy gesture caused
That slender rod to snap.

Love came along. Love came along.
Then you. And now it's ended.
Tomorrow I shall tidy up
And get the radio mended.

The Orange

At lunchtime I bought a huge orange –
The size of it made us all laugh.
I peeled it and shared it with Robert and Dave –
They got quarters and I had a half.

And that orange, it made me so happy,
As ordinary things often do
Just lately. The shopping. A walk in the park.
This is peace and contentment. It's new.

The rest of the day was quite easy.
I did all the jobs on my list
And enjoyed them and had some time over.
I love you. I'm glad I exist.

Some More Light Verse

You have to try. You see a shrink.
You learn a lot. You read. You think.
You struggle to improve your looks.
You meet some men. You write some books.
You eat good food. You give up junk.
You do not smoke. You don't get drunk.
You take up yoga, walk and swim.
And nothing works. The outlook's grim.
You don't know what to do. You cry.
You're running out of things to try.

You blow your nose. You see the shrink.
You walk. You give up food and drink.
You fall in love. You make a plan.
You struggle to improve your man.
And nothing works. The outlook's grim.
You go to yoga, cry and swim.
You eat and drink. You give up looks.
You struggle to improve your books.
You cannot see the point. You sigh.
You do not smoke. You have to try.

As Sweet

It's all because we're so alike –
Twin souls, we two.
We smile at the expression, yes,
And know it's true.

I told the shrink. He gave our love
A different name.
But he can call it what he likes –
It's still the same.

I long to see you, hear your voice,
My narcissistic object-choice.

Loss

The day he moved out was terrible –
That evening she went through hell.
His absence wasn't a problem
But the corkscrew had gone as well.

Two Cures for Love

1. Don't see him. Don't phone or write a letter.
2. The easy way: get to know him better.

Favourite

When they ask me, 'Who's your favourite poet?'
I'd better not mention you,
Though you certainly are my favourite poet
And I like your poems too.

Another Unfortunate Choice

I think I am in love with A. E. Housman,
Which puts me in a worse-than-usual fix.
No woman ever stood a chance with Housman
And he's been dead since 1936.

Letter

Alone too much this week,
I'm in my poet mode –
Awake at half past five and writing,
Dozing on the sofa-bed by ten.

You're there, of course, my absent angel,
But for once we don't make love
Or even talk. You have been working
In another room and then

You come in, carrying a blanket,
And cover me while I'm asleep.
It's cold today. I need the blanket.
You do it over and over again.

Nine-Line Triolet

Here's a fine mess we got ourselves into,
My angel, my darling, true love of my heart
Et cetera. Must stop it but I can't begin to.
Here's a fine mess we got ourselves into –
Both in a spin with nowhere to spin to,
Bound by the old rules in life and in art.
Here's a fine mess we got ourselves into,
(I'll curse every rule in the book as we part),
My angel, my darling, true love of my heart.

Magnetic

i spell it out on this fridge door
you are so wonderful
i even like th way you snor

On a Country Bus

The fat boy in the seat across the aisle
Is reading *Dragons of Autumn Twilight Volume One*
And listening to something dreadful on his Walkman.
Sometimes I wish I needed books and music
More than I do. Today I don't need anything –
I didn't want my lunch. And, more remarkable,
I feel quite tolerant about the tinny buzzing
From his earphones. I shall just sit back
And think about the things you say and do
And nothing else. The journey takes almost an hour.

After the Lunch

On Waterloo Bridge, where we said our goodbyes,
The weather conditions bring tears to my eyes.
I wipe them away with a black woolly glove
And try not to notice I've fallen in love.

On Waterloo Bridge I am trying to think:
This is nothing. You're high on the charm and the drink.
But the juke-box inside me is playing a song
That says something different. And when was it wrong?

On Waterloo Bridge with the wind in my hair
I am tempted to skip. *You're a fool.* I don't care.
The head does its best but the heart is the boss –
I admit it before I am halfway across.

In the Rhine Valley

Die Farben der Bäume sind schön
And the sky's and the river's blue-greys
And the *Burg*, almost lost in the haze.

You're patient. You help me to learn
And you smile as I practise the phrase,
'*Die Farben der Bäume sind schön.*'

October. The year's on the turn –
It will take us our separate ways
But the sun shines. And we have two days.
Die Farben der Bäume sind schön.

Valentine

My heart has made its mind up
And I'm afraid it's you.
Whatever you've got lined up,
My heart has made its mind up
And if you can't be signed up
This year, next year will do.
My heart has made its mind up
And I'm afraid it's you.

Faint Praise

Size isn't everything. It's what you do
That matters, darling, and you do quite well
In some respects. Credit where credit's due –
You work, you're literate, you rarely smell.
Small men can be aggressive, people say,
But you are often genial and kind,
As long as you can have things all your way
And I comply, and do not speak my mind.
You look all right. I've never been disgusted
By paunchiness. Who wants some skinny youth?
My friends have warned me that you can't be trusted
But I protest I've heard you tell the truth.
Nobody's perfect. Now and then, my pet,
You're almost human. You could make it yet.

I Worry

I worry about you –
So long since we spoke.
Love, are you downhearted,
Dispirited, broke?

I worry about you.
I can't sleep at night.
Are you sad? Are you lonely?
Or are you all right?

They say that men suffer,
As badly, as long.
I worry, I worry,
In case they are wrong.

So Much Depends

*'And another thing: I gave in far too easily
over William Carlos Williams.'*

I can't remember what you said about him.
Was it thumbs down or the big hurrah?
When it comes to William Carlos Williams,
I've no idea what your opinions are.

I argued with you? That seems most unlikely.
I may have looked attentive for a while.
I've searched my head for William Carlos Williams
And there is very little in the file.

I'll fight with you about important issues
Like who should buy the bread or clean the sink
But when it comes to William Carlos Williams,
Dearest, I really don't mind what you think.

Yes, mutter darkly, 'Well, perhaps you ought to,'
And fire offensive weapons from those eyes.
When it comes to William Carlos Williams,
It won't do any good. I will not rise.

A Christmas Poem

At Christmas little children sing and merry bells jingle,
The cold winter air makes our hands and faces tingle
And happy families go to church and cheerily they mingle
And the whole business is unbelievably dreadful, if you're single.

The New Regime

Yes, I agree. We'll pull ourselves together.
We eat too much. We're always getting pissed.
It's not a bad idea to find out whether
We like each other sober. Let's resist.
I've got the Perrier and the carrot-grater,
I'll look on a Scotch or a pudding as a crime.
We all have to be sensible sooner or later
But don't let's be sensible all the time.

No more thinking about a second bottle
And saying 'What the hell?' and giving in.
Tomorrow I'll be jogging at full throttle
To make myself successful, rich and thin.
A healthy life's a great rejuvenator
But, God, it's going to be an uphill climb.
We all have to be sensible sooner or later
But don't let's be sensible all the time.

The conversation won't be half as trivial –
You'll hold forth on the issues of the day –
And, when our evenings aren't quite so convivial,
You'll start remembering the things I say.
Oh, see if you can catch the eye of the waiter
And order me a double vodka and lime.
We all have to be sensible sooner or later
But I refuse to be sensible all the time.

New Season

No coats today. Buds bulge on chestnut trees,
and on the doorstep of a big, old house
a young man stands and plays his flute.

I watch the silver notes fly up
and circle in blue sky above the traffic,
travelling where they will.

And suddenly this paving-stone
midway between my front door and the bus stop
is a starting-point.

From here I can go anywhere I choose.

Legacy

She left two Premium Bonds
And what remained of that week's pension,
Her clothes, photographs, and china ornaments
We'd given her as children.

Also the crocheted mats
She made as wedding presents,
Babies' shawls, the suit
My teddy bear still wears,
And fifty pairs of woolly socks
In drawers all over England.

Names

She was Eliza for a few weeks
When she was a baby –
Eliza Lily. Soon it changed to Lil.

Later she was Miss Steward in the baker's shop
And then 'my love', 'my darling', Mother.

Widowed at thirty, she went back to work
As Mrs Hand. Her daughter grew up,
Married and gave birth.

Now she was Nanna. 'Everybody
Calls me Nanna,' she would say to visitors.
And so they did – friends, tradesmen, the doctor.

In the geriatric ward
They used the patients' Christian names.
'Lil,' we said, 'or Nanna,'
But it wasn't in her file
And for those last bewildered weeks
She was Eliza once again.

For My Sister, Emigrating

You've left with me
the things you couldn't take
or bear to give away –
books, records and a biscuit-tin
that Nanna gave you.

It's old and dirty
and the lid won't fit.
Standing in a corner of my room,
quite useless, it's as touching
as a once-loved toy.

Yes, sentimental now –
but if you'd stayed,
we would have quarrelled
just the same as ever,
found excuses not to phone.

We never learn. We've grown up
struggling, frightened
that the family would drown us,
only giving in to love
when someone's dead or gone.

Leaving

for Dick and Afkham

Next summer? The summer after?
With luck we've a few more years
Of sunshine and drinking and laughter
And airports and goodbyes and tears.

The Uncertainty of the Poet

'The Tate Gallery yesterday announced that it had paid £1 million for a Giorgio de Chirico masterpiece, The Uncertainty of the Poet. *It depicts a torso and a bunch of bananas.'*
— Guardian, 2 April 1985

I am a poet.
I am very fond of bananas.

I am bananas.
I am very fond of a poet.

I am a poet of bananas.
I am very fond,

A fond poet of 'I am, I am' –
Very bananas,

Fond of 'Am I bananas,
Am I?' – a very poet.

Bananas of a poet!
Am I fond? Am I very?

Poet bananas! I am.
I am fond of a 'very'.

I am of very fond bananas.
Am I a poet?

Poem Composed in Santa Barbara

The poets talk. They talk a lot.
They talk of T. S. Eliot.
One is anti. One is pro.
How hard they think! How much they know!
They're happy. A cicada sings.
We women talk of other things.

The Poet's Song

tune: 'The Lord Chancellor's Song' from Iolanthe

after W. S. Gilbert

When I started to write as a very young man
(Said I to myself – said I),
I'll always produce the best work that I can
(Said I to myself – said I).
I've devoted myself to the life of the mind
And I shan't drop my standards at all, should I find
That my mortgage repayments have fallen behind
(Said I to myself – said I).

If I get a call from the BBC
(Said I to myself – said I),
I'll be pithy and terse and to hell with the fee
(Said I to myself – said I).
They pay by the minute. It wouldn't be hard
To run the stuff off by the foot or the yard
And forget it tomorrow. I'll be on my guard,
(Said I to myself – said I).

I shan't include stanzas I'm iffy about
(Said I to myself – said I),
Or use a refrain just to pad the thing out
(Said I to myself – said I).
If it's metrically wonky, I shan't send it in
And hope that the Muse will forgive me my sin
And that the producer has ears made of tin,
(Said I to myself – said I).

It's better to be conscientious and poor
(Said I to myself – said I),
All poets abide by this maxim, I'm sure
(Said I to myself – said I),
And that's why you never hear second-rate stuff,
A trifle long-winded or boring or duff
And scream at your radio set, 'That's enough!'
(Said I to myself – said I).

Tumps

Don't ask him the time of day. He won't know it,
For he's the abstracted sort.
In fact, he's a typically useless male poet.
We'll call him a tump for short.

A tump isn't punctual or smart or efficient,
He probably can't drive a car
Or follow a map, though he's very proficient
At finding his way to the bar.

He may have great talent, and not just for writing –
For drawing, or playing the drums.
But don't let him loose on accounts – that's inviting
Disaster. A tump can't do sums.

He cannot get organised. Just watch him try it
And you'll see a frustrated man.
But some tumps (and these are the worst ones) deny it
And angrily tell you they can.

I used to be close to a tump who would bellow
'You think I can't add two and two!'
And get even crosser when, smiling and mellow,
I answered, 'You're quite right. I do.'

Women poets are businesslike, able,
Good drivers, and right on the ball,
And some of us still know our seven times table.
We're not like the tumps. Not at all.

The Cricketing Versions

for Simon Rae

'There isn't much cricket in the Cromwell play.'
— overheard at a dinner-party

There isn't much cricket in *Hamlet* either,
There isn't much cricket in *Lear*.
I don't think there's any in *Paradise Lost** —
I haven't a copy right here.

But I like to imagine the cricketing versions —
Laertes goes out to bat
And instead of claiming a palpable hit,
The prince gives a cry of 'Howzat!'

While elsewhere the nastier daughters of Lear
(Both women cricketers) scheme
To keep their talented younger sister
Out of the England team,

And up in the happy realms of light
When Satan is out (great catch)
His team and the winners sit down together
For sandwiches after the match.

Although there are some English writers
Who feature the red leather ball,
You could make a long list of the plays and the books
In which there's no cricket at all.

*Apparently there is. 'Chaos umpire sits, / And by decision more embroils the fray.' *Paradise Lost*, Book II, lines 907–8.

To be perfectly honest, I like them that way –
The absence of cricket is fine.
But if you prefer work that includes it, please note
That now there's some cricket in mine.

Another Christmas Poem

Bloody Christmas, here again.
Let us raise a loving cup:
Peace on earth, goodwill to men,
And make them do the washing-up.

19th Christmas Poem

for Nicholas Shakespeare and John Coldstream

Christmas is coming.
The phone rings and I curse.
Literary editor.
Seasonal verse.

Big deal. Big chance
To sell them a rhyme.
They never publish poetry
Except at Christmastime.

Christmas is coming,
Last week in September.
Can you let us have it
By the second of November?

Light and clean and printable –
You know the kind of thing.
If you want a Christmas bonus,
Now's the time to sing.

Christmas is coming.
Books of the year.
I re-read *Persuasion*,
War and Peace, *King Lear*.

We don't count that stuff.
It isn't what we mean.
We thought you were part
Of the literary scene.

Christmas is coming.
Better play the game.
Mother reads the *Telegraph*.
She likes to see my name.

Last year it made her
Happy as a bird
To find her elder daughter
Under Douglas Hurd.

Christmas is coming.
Here's my Christmas song –
Light and clean and printable
And forty lines long.

Dear Dial-a-Poet,
Hope it will do.
Please to pay without delay
And God bless you.

Reflections on a Royalty Statement

They've given me a number
So they will know it's me
And not some other Wendy Cope
(They publish two or three).
When I go to see them
I wear a number-plate
Or sometimes I salute and say,
'032838.'

What a lot of authors!
The digits make it clear
That publishers are busy –
You can phone them once a year
But it isn't done to grumble
If the cheque's a little late:
'Look, we've other things to think about,
032838.'

Sometimes they give a party
And all the numbers go.
'It's 027564!'
'036040!'
'Hey, have you seen 014's book?
You're right. He's second-rate.
But even so he's better than
032838.'

We're one big happy family
(My eyes are getting runny)
And, what is more, if we do well
They give us pocket-money!

Some publishers are terrible
But mine are really great.
OK? Can this go in my book? –
032838.

An Argument with Wordsworth

'Poetry . . . takes its origin from emotion recollected in tranquillity'
  – Preface to the *Lyrical Ballads*

People are always quoting that and all of them seem to agree
And it's probably most unwise to admit that it's different for me.
I have emotion – no one who knows me could fail to detect it –
But there's a serious shortage of tranquillity in which to recollect it.
So this is my contribution to the theoretical debate:
Sometimes poetry is emotion recollected in a highly emotional state.

Variation on Belloc's 'Fatigue'

I hardly ever tire of love or rhyme –
That's why I'm poor and have a rotten time.

Bloody Men

Bloody men are like bloody buses –
You wait for about a year
And as soon as one approaches your stop
Two or three others appear.

You look at them flashing their indicators,
Offering you a ride.
You're trying to read the destinations,
You haven't much time to decide.

If you make a mistake, there is no turning back.
Jump off, and you'll stand there and gaze
While the cars and the taxis and lorries go by
And the minutes, the hours, the days.

Men and Their Boring Arguments

One man on his own can be quite good fun
But don't go drinking with two –
They'll probably have an argument
And take no notice of you.

What makes men so tedious
Is the need to show off and compete.
They'll bore you to death for hours and hours
Before they'll admit defeat.

It often happens at dinner-parties
Where brother disputes with brother
And we can't even talk among ourselves
Because we're not next to each other.

Some men like to argue with women –
Don't give them a chance to begin.
You won't be allowed to change the subject
Until you have given in.

A man with the bit between his teeth
Will keep you up half the night
And the only way to get some sleep
Is to say, 'I expect you're right.'

I expect you're right, my dearest love.
I expect you're right, my friend.
These boring arguments make no difference
To anything in the end.

Noises in the Night

Why are men so good at sleeping?
Is it just the drink?
While we're tossing, turning, weeping,
Why are they so good at sleeping?
Snoring, whistling, grunting, beeping –
No one else can get a wink.
Why are men so good at sleeping?
Is it just the drink?

Advice to Young Women

When you're a spinster of forty,
You're reduced to considering bids
From husbands inclined to be naughty
And divorcés obsessed with their kids.

So perhaps you should wed in a hurry,
But that has its drawbacks as well.
The answer? There's no need to worry –
Whatever you do, life is hell.

Variation on a Lennon and McCartney Song

Love, love, love,
Love, love, love,
Love, love, love,
Dooby doo dooby doo,
All you need is love,
Dooby dooby doo,
All you need is love,
Dooby dooby doo,
All you need is love, love
Or, failing that, alcohol.

Exchange of Letters

'Man who is a serious novel would like to hear from a woman who is a poem'
— classified advertisement, *New York Review of Books*

Dear Serious Novel,

I am a terse, assured lyric with impeccable rhythmic flow, some apt and original metaphors, and a music that is all my own. Some people say I am beautiful.

My vital statistics are eighteen lines, divided into three-line stanzas, with an average of four words per line.

My first husband was a cheap romance; the second was *Wisdens Cricketers' Almanac*. Most of the men I meet nowadays are autobiographies, but a substantial minority are books about photography or trains.

I have always hoped for a relationship with an upmarket work of fiction. Please write and tell me more about yourself.

Yours intensely,
Song of the First Snowdrop

Dear Song of the First Snowdrop,

Many thanks for your letter. You sound like just the kind of poem I am hoping to find. I've always preferred short, lyrical women to the kind who go on for page after page.

I am an important 150,000-word comment on the dreams and dilemmas of twentieth-century Man. It took six years to attain my present weight and stature but all the twenty-seven publishers I have so far approached have failed to understand me. I have my share of sex and violence and a very good joke in chapter nine, but to no avail. I am sustained by the belief that I am ahead of my time.

Let's meet as soon as possible. I am longing for you to read me from cover to cover and get to know my every word.

                Yours impatiently,
                Death of the Zeitgeist

A Green Song

to sing at the bottle-bank

One green bottle,
Drop it in the bank.
Ten green bottles,
What a lot we drank.
Heaps of bottles
And yesterday's a blank
But we'll save the planet,
Tinkle, tinkle, clank!

We've got bottles –
Nice, percussive trash.
Bags of bottles
Cleaned us out of cash.
Empty bottles,
We love to hear them smash
And we'll save the planet,
Tinkle, tinkle, crash!

The Concerned Adolescent

Our planet spins around the sun
in its oval-shaped orbit
like a moth circling a bright, hot, golden-yellow lightbulb.

Look at this beautiful, lovely
blue and green and white jewel
shining against the dark black sky.
It is doomed.

On another planet somewhere far away in the galaxy
beings are discussing the problems of Earth.
'It is a wonderful world,' says their leader,
'It has roaring oceans filled with many kinds of fishes,
it has green meadows bedecked with white and yellow flowers,
its trees have twisting roots and fruitful, abundant branches.
But it is doomed.

'The problem with this lovely, beautiful world, you see,
is the inhabitants, known as HUMAN BEINGS.
Human beings will not live in peace and love
and care for the little helpless creatures who share the planet
    with them.

They pollute the world, they kill and eat the animals.
Everywhere there is blood and the stench of death.
Human beings make war and hate one another.
They do not understand their young, they reject their ideals,
they make them come home early from the disco.
They are doomed.'

Soon a great explosion, a terrible cloud
will wipe out all the life on this planet,
including those people who do not see how important my
   poem is.
They are certainly doomed.

Goldfish Nation

by Jason Strugnell

In the pond
There are no bombs, no guns, no bullets.
There is no property and no television.
The pond is the territory not of humans
But of the goldfish.
He is better than you.

Goldfish play.
They do not work.
They do not set the alarm clock
And get up at half past seven
And get on a crowded commuter train
And go to the office.
They are playful creatures.
Goldfish play.
Their games are non-competitive –
Swimming into a space and twisting,
Looking for another space.
All day long it's like PE
In a progressive infant school.

Goldfish are intelligent.
They answer to their names.
Go out and sprinkle
Just a pinch of fish food
As you call to them
And see them rising from the muddy depths
To greet you. Sunshine. Goldy.

Flipper. Bertrand Russell. Maharishi. Name your goldfish
After holy men and sages.
It is appropriate.

'Look on the goldfish,' say the Inkuwala,
'And be at peace.'

The Watatooki of Wideawake Bay
Have a different saying:
'He who contemplates the goldfish
Will grow wiser than a frog.'

Albert Eames of Norwood Fish Society
Believes that his goldfish, Lucky,
Is a bringer of good fortune.
'It's a well-known fact,' he says,
'That many goldfish owners in South London
Have won prizes with their Premium Bonds.'

The sex life of the goldfish, it has to be admitted,
Is somewhat less exciting
Than the mating of whales.

The fact is goldfish do not have a sex life.
They breed without physical contact,
Shedding enormous quantities of sperm and eggs
Into the water.

Hundreds and hundreds of sperm are attracted
To each egg
And each one tries to bore its way through the shell
But only one succeeds in doing so.

After fertilisation, the egg faces tremendous hazards,
Including the danger of being eaten
By the very fish who gave it life.

But some survive. The fry swim. They eat.
They grow. Their scales ripen to gold.
And they play.

Like Buddhists,
Goldfish are disinclined
To get into an argument.
They do not discuss interest rates
Or debate the ordination of women.
On these matters they seem to have no opinion.
They prefer to play.

Ludic, aureate creatures,
Silently chanting *Om*,
Gazing at reality with round, unblinking eyes.
Water-angels, glinting in the sunlight.

It's obvious that goldfish are better than people.
Goldfish are better than you.

Written after the publication of *Whale Nation* by Heathcote Williams.

Roger Bear's Football Poems

Three cheers for Spurs!
They beat Stoke!
Glad I'm a football fan.
Glad I'm a bloke.

*

Who beat Liverpool
Then beat them again?
Tottenham Hotspur –
A bunch of real men.

*

Tottenham lost
And I am sad.
Sometimes it's difficult
Being a lad.

*

Spurs beat Newcastle,
Just like I reckoned.
Spurs are brilliant
And now they are second.

*

Will they beat Everton?
We'll have to see.
Please get a ticket
For Wendy and me.

Roger Bear's Philosophical Pantoum

I stare at the ceiling.
I look very wise.
Up with thinking and feeling
And stuff exercise.

I look very wise –
I am keen on reflection
And stuff. Exercise?
I prefer introspection.

I am keen on reflection,
Like old Aristotle –
I prefer introspection
To hitting the bottle.

Like old Aristotle,
I rarely descend
To hitting the bottle –
My arms will not bend.

I rarely descend
As far as the floor.
My arms will not bend –
Sometimes life is a bore.

As far as the floor –
A long way to fall.
Sometimes life is a bore.
I gaze at the wall.

A long way to fall –
I stay on the quilt.
I gaze at the wall,
I wrestle with guilt.

I lie on the quilt
On my comfortable bed.
I wrestle with guilt
Until I am fed.

On my comfortable bed,
I stare at the ceiling
Until I am fed
Up with thinking and feeling.

Strugnell's Evangelical Songs

I

to the tune 'Daisy Bell'

Jesus, Jesus! Who is on Jesus' side?
Wear His colours, sing out His name with pride!
Supporters of His eleven
Are sure to get to Heaven.
Up in the sky, while others fry,
We'll be winners who never died!

2

Jesus came to work with me today.
He kept me calm and happy all the way.
He didn't make a fuss
About the crowded bus
Or moan about conditions, hours and pay.

Jesus came to work, He came along.
I carried out my duties with a song.
I went the extra mile
And wore a Christian smile –
The smile that says, 'I know I can't be wrong.'

Jesus came to work, He came to lunch
With me and Tony and the usual bunch.
I bought a round of beers
And said, 'To Jesus. Cheers!'
And Tony laughed and, Lord, that was the crunch.

Jesus told me, 'Turn the other cheek.'
And so I did, but first I had to speak.
I muttered, 'Just you wait
Till you get to Heaven's gate,
You jerk.' Then I went back to being meek.

Jesus came to work, my feet were swift,
My spirits kept on soaring like the lift.
Being saved is bliss –
It helps me write like this.
Thank you, Lord, for my poetic gift.

3
for Fraser Steel

When I went out shopping,
I said a little prayer:
'Jesus, help me park the car
For you are everywhere.'

Jesus, in His goodness and grace,
Jesus found me a parking space
In a very convenient place.
Sound the horn and praise Him!

His eternal car-park
Is hidden from our eyes.
Trust in Him and you will have
A space beyond the skies.

Jesus, in His goodness and grace,
Wants to find you a parking space.
Ask Him now to reserve a place.
Sound the horn and praise Him!

from Strugnell Lunaire

The silver moon pours down her light.
I drink it in with thirsty eyes.
I'd rather have another pint of lager
But all the pubs are closed.
The poet must drink deep of life
To find poetic ecstasy.
The silver moon pours down her light.
I drink it in with thirsty eyes.
Tonight I am intoxicated
And every night it is the same.
I wander down the beauteous high street
And, if the weather isn't cloudy,
The silver moon pours down her light.

The composer Colin Matthews asked me to write parodies of the words of some modern song cycles. This one was inspired by the words (by Albert Giraud) that Schoenberg used in *Pierrot lunaire*.

the homeless hammer

I FURIOUS OBJECTS

the sick umbrella underneath the council chamber
and a cow in the washbasin
I rage, a cushion in captivity
the teapot will not break its bonds

II SECOND SIGHT IN BROCKWELL PARK

my toenails listen
to the soggy grass
mankind – a wind-tossed ice-cream wrapper
life – a melancholy bus
I walk, I have these visions
and they are really quite depressing

III SOLITARY BEER-MAT

the clock has lost its knitting, it needs a woman
eyes in the paving-stones are weeping
to see pink elephants in Norwood Road

Inspired by René Char's 'Le Marteau sans maître', set
to music by Pierre Boulez.

Ahead of My Time

poems for musical performance by Jason Strugnell

CLOUDS

Sprinkle the air around you
with short, quiet sounds

Make more and more raindrops
until your co-players

are drenched

Let the intervals between sounds
grow longer

When you have finished raining
hold still
Loom

PERPLEXITY

Gaze into the eyes
of a co-player

At irregular intervals
scratch your head

WELTSCHMERZ

Play and/or sing

extremely long quiet sounds

When the tedium
has become unbearable

scream

QUARTET FOR FOUR BEER DRINKERS

From your pint glass
take a swig of beer
whenever you feel like it

When you are not actually drinking
strike your glass
with an implement

sometimes quietly
sometimes loudly

Let there be silences between your attacks

Continue
until all four glasses are empty

Inspired by the works of Karlheinz Stockhausen

English Weather

January's grey and slushy,
February's chill and drear,
March is wild and wet and windy,
April seldom brings much cheer.
In May, a day or two of sunshine,
Three or four in June, perhaps.
July is usually filthy,
August skies are open taps.
In September things start dying,
Then comes cold October mist.
November we make plans to spend
The best part of December pissed.

Serious Concerns

'She is witty and unpretentious, which is both her strength and her limitation.'
 — ROBERT O'BRIEN *in the* Spectator, *25 October 1986*

I'm going to try and overcome my limitation —
Away with sloth!
Now should I work at being less witty? Or more
 pretentious?
Or both?

'They [Roger McGough and Brian Patten] have something in common with her, in that they all write to amuse.'
 — *Ibid.*

Write to amuse? What an appalling suggestion!
I write to make people anxious and miserable
 and to worsen their indigestion.

Kindness to Animals

If I went vegetarian
And didn't eat lambs for dinner,
I think I'd be a better person
And also thinner.

But the lamb is not endangered
And at least I can truthfully say
I have never, ever eaten a barn owl,
So perhaps I am OK.

This poem was commissioned by the editor of *The Orange Dove of Fiji*, an anthology for the benefit of the World Wide Fund for Nature. It was rejected as unsuitable.

Does She Like Word Games?

She likes sonnets but she doesn't like poems.
She doesn't like sestinas or whisky.
No, she doesn't like limericks either, or water, or
    television or cats.

She likes sweets but she doesn't like eating.
She likes apples too.

She likes Schumann but she doesn't like Stravinsky.
She's fond of jazz and piccolos.
She dislikes songs.

She has a warm regard for Russian dancers,
Spanish jugglers, little people,
Especially if they're green.

She likes especially as well. And as well
For that matter. And for that matter.
She can't stand Shakespeare.

Among her favourites are spelling bees,
Football, the Book of Common Prayer.
And there are great loves –
James Russell Lowell, the Mississippi.

She likes sonnets but she doesn't like the sky.

She doesn't like repetition.
She doesn't like repetition.

She doesn't like endings.

UNCOLLECTED POEMS

— 1986–1991 —

Lauda

by Harry Oberländer

They became angels. And their wings could lift
The burden of the days they'd left behind.
They gave themselves to the mysterious gift
Entirely, and forgot that they could wound.

Blue mountains swam into the evenings. Still
A few nights left – a mercy and a danger.
The lake was large and silent. Who could tell
If something more than chance had brought this stranger?

Today we see them, each a pale survivor,
Earthbound, mortal, here and everywhere.
Their grief is quiet and their flight is over.
They are apart. They've tumbled through the air.

Translated from the German by the author and Wendy Cope.

Sonnet

*'If human beings ever communicate with one another,
it is through poetry.'*
— C. H. SISSON in a radio programme *c*.1989

A German dictionary on my knee,
I try to read a poem. It is tough.
The literal meaning makes no sense to me.
Well, what did I expect? It's highbrow stuff
And I am not at all sure that I'd get it
If you had written it in English. Still,
I struggle on. I do not want to let it
Defeat me, though quite probably it will.
To reach you now I have to fight my way
Through tangled undergrowth until I start
To hear your voice more clearly, as you say
What's on your mind and what is in your heart.
Perhaps, though I'm not with you anymore,
I'll know you better than I did before.

You and I

We loved each other, you and I.
This, it seems, is how it ends:
Years of silence. Then we die.

There is nothing left to try.
We can't make peace. We can't be friends.
We loved each other, you and I.

Nothing left to do but cry
As the barrier descends.
We loved each other. Love, goodbye.

In a Clifftop Shelter at Falmouth

Grey mist and drizzle everywhere.
Beyond the glass partition
two old ladies, shapeless
in coats and plastic headgear
talk and smile contentedly.
I cannot understand.

I make myself imagine coming here
when I am their age. I shall sit
on this seat and remember everything –
today, how heavy love felt
as I trudged up hill,
and how it all turned out.

Twenty or thirty years.
No way of knowing
what you'll be to me by then –
my love, my friend, a distant incident –
or if the interval, seen from the other side,
will look as grey.

They're on their feet,
the two old ladies, pointing
as the first yacht rounds the headland
and a whole flotilla, red,
white, blue – a line of bunting –
slowly unwinds across the bay.

Closing the Anthology

Closing the anthology, I wonder if it's time
To throw away the green and orange jacket,
Gaudy clothing of its youth,

And let it be a sober adult, following
Its ancestors into the navy, gold braid
Gleaming on a flawless uniform.

In time it will grow shabby, the binding slack,
And I shall need spectacles to read it. Later,
Brown spots will appear on the pages,

And someone, in a dusty shop, will open it
At the fly-leaf. I wish I'd written my name
More carefully, in Indian ink.

In Demand

He couldn't be nicer if I were a king.
All the same, I suspect he's a jerk.
Like most of them, this man is after one thing
And unfortunately it's my work.

Postcard Poem

Will they do this, I wonder,
With verse of mine or yours,
When we are six feet under
And deaf to all applause?

We bring home little bacon
En route for that long night
And when the profit's taken
We're out of copyright.

Written on the back of a postcard. A quatrain by Housman is printed on the front of the card. This poem can be sung to the hymn tune 'Aurelia' ('The church's one foundation').

A Contented Poem

for Desmond Clarke

It's very dark inside a book.
Silent poems, side by side,
Long for light and readers' eyes
To tell them that they haven't died.

I do not envy them. Though I
May never be in print at all,
I like it here inside this frame,
Hanging on an office wall.

The late Desmond Clarke, former sales and marketing director of Faber and Faber, asked me for a poem to put on his office wall. I think he meant a handwritten copy of an old poem but I decided to write a new one.

Where Do You Get Your Ideas From?

They used to be delivered by the milkman –
'Two pints, please, and a brilliant idea.'
But they began to vanish from the doorstep
And I was only getting three a year.

I tried the shop, the big one down in Norwood,
I-D-R-Mart. I wandered down an aisle
Where Nature was displayed in great abundance:
Trees, flowers, sunsets, dead sheep (by the pile) –

The usual stuff. I hurried past Domestic,
Domestic Pets (BE TENDER! MOURN YOUR CAT!),
And Politics (GREAT VALUE! EEZEE TARGETS!),
And paused at Love. But I was sick of that.

It's difficult. It's worse than buying trousers.
They have to be just right. They're hard to find.
No luck for weeks. Then someone asks a question
And gives me one I like. How very kind.

On Learning the Correct Pronunciation of the Name of a Poetic Form

in memory of Gavin Ewart 1916–95

I always assumed it was French
But Gavin rhymes it with violet
So I will defer to the bench.
I always assumed it was French –
Tree-oh-lay. It will be quite a wrench
To adjust to pronouncing it triolet.
I always assumed it was French
But Gavin rhymes it with violet.

IF I DON'T KNOW

— 2001 —

I

By the Round Pond

You watch yourself. You watch the watcher too –
A ghostly figure on the garden wall.
And one of you is her, and one is you,
If either one of you exists at all.

How strange to be the one behind a face,
To have a name and know that it is yours,
To be in this particular green place,
To see a snail advance, to see it pause.

You sit quite still and wonder when you'll go.
It could be now. Or now. Or now. You stay.
Who's making up the plot? You'll never know.
Minute after minute swims away.

The Christmas Life

*'If you don't have a real tree, you don't bring
the Christmas life into the house.'*
— JOSEPHINE MACKINNON, aged 8

Bring in a tree, a young Norwegian spruce,
Bring hyacinths that rooted in the cold.
Bring winter jasmine as its buds unfold –
Bring the Christmas life into this house.

Bring red and green and gold, bring things that shine,
Bring candlesticks and music, food and wine.
Bring in your memories of Christmas past.
Bring in your tears for all that you have lost.

Bring in the shepherd boy, the ox and ass,
Bring in the stillness of an icy night,
Bring in a birth, of hope and love and light.
Bring the Christmas life into this house.

30th December

At first I'm startled by the sound of bicycles
Above my head. And then I see them, two swans
Flying in to their runway behind the reeds.

The bridge is slippery, the grass so sodden
That water seeps into my shoes. But now
The sun has come out and everything is calm
And beautiful as the end of a hangover.

Christmas was a muddle
Of turkey bones and muted quarrelling.

The visitors have left.
Solitary walkers smile and tell each other
That the day is wonderful.

If only this could be Christmas now –
These shining meadows,
The hum of huge wings in the sky.

If I Don't Know

for Louise Kerr

If I don't know how to be thankful enough
for the clusters of white blossom

on our mock orange, which has grown tall
and graceful, come into its own

like a new star just out of ballet school,
and if I don't know what to do

about those spires of sky-blue delphinium,
then what about the way they look together?

And what about the roses, or just one of them –
that solid pinky-peachy bloom

that hollows towards its heart? Outrageous.
I could crush it to bits.

A photograph? A dance to summer?
I sit on the swing and cry.

The rose. The gardenful. The evening light.
It's nine o'clock and I can still see everything.

Haiku: Looking Out of the Back Bedroom Window without My Glasses

What's that amazing
new lemon-yellow flower?
Oh yes, a football.

Idyll

after U. A. Fanthorpe

We'll be in our garden on a summer evening,
Eating pasta, drinking white wine.

We won't talk all the time. I'll sit back,
Contemplating shadows on the red-brick path,

And marvel at the way it all turned out.
That yellow begonia. Our gabled house.

Later we'll stroll through Kingsgate Park.
My leg won't hurt, and we'll go home the long way.

Asked to imagine heaven, I see us there,
The way we have been, the way we sometimes are.

Being Boring

'May you live in interesting times.'
— Chinese curse

If you ask me 'What's new?', I have nothing to say
Except that the garden is growing.
I had a slight cold but it's better today.
I'm content with the way things are going.
Yes, he is the same as he usually is,
Still eating and sleeping and snoring.
I get on with my work. He gets on with his.
I know this is all very boring.

There was drama enough in my turbulent past:
Tears and passion – I've used up a tankful.
No news is good news, and long may it last.
If nothing much happens, I'm thankful.
A happier cabbage you never did see,
My vegetable spirits are soaring.
If you're after excitement, steer well clear of me.
I want to go on being boring.

I don't go to parties. Well, what are they for,
If you don't need to find a new lover?
You drink and you listen and drink a bit more
And you take the next day to recover.
Someone to stay home with was all my desire
And, now that I've found a safe mooring,
I've just one ambition in life: I aspire
To go on and on being boring.

Fireworks Poems

*commissioned by the Salisbury Festival
to be displayed in fireworks*

I

Faster and faster,
They vanish into darkness:
Our years together.

II

Write it in fire across the night:
Some men are more or less all right.

Timekeeping

Late home for supper,
He mustn't seem drunk.
'The pob cluck', he begins,
And knows he is sunk.

Song

My love got in the car
And sat on my banana,
My unobserved banana
And my organic crisps.

We spoke of life and love,
His rump on my banana,
My hidden, soft banana
And my forgotten crisps.

He kissed me more than once
As he sat on that banana,
That newly squashed banana
And those endangered crisps.

We looked up at the stars –
Beneath him, my banana,
My saved-from-lunch banana
And my delicious crisps.

At last I dropped him off
And noticed the banana –
Alas, a ruined banana
And sadly damaged crisps.

You'd think he would have felt
A fairly large banana
And, if not the banana,
The lumpy bag of crisps.

But he's the kind of man
Who'll sit on a banana
For hours. Watch your banana
And guard your bag of crisps.

He waved goodbye and smiled,
Benign as a banana.
'I love you, daft banana,'
Said I, and ate the crisps.

On a Train

The book I've been reading
rests on my knee. You sleep.

It's beautiful out there –
fields, little lakes and winter trees
in February sunlight,
every car park a shining mosaic.

Long, radiant minutes,
your hand in my hand,
still warm, still warm.

Present

On the flyleaf
of my confirmation present:
'To Wendy with love
from Nanna. Psalm 98.'

I looked it up, eventually –
Cantate Domino.
I knew the first two verses
and skimmed the rest.

Thirty-five years afterwards,
at evensong on Day 19
the choir sings Nanna's psalm.
At last, I pay attention

to the words she chose.
*O sing unto the Lord
a new song.* Nanna,
it is just what I wanted.

Postcards

commissioned for broadcast by BBC World Service

At first I sent you a postcard
From every city I went to.
Grüsse aus Bath, aus Birmingham,
Aus Rotterdam, aus Tel Aviv.
Mit Liebe. Cards from you arrived
In English, with many commas.
Hope, you're fine and still alive,
Says one from Hong Kong. By that time
We weren't writing quite as often.

Now we're nearly nine years away
From the lake and the blue mountains,
And the room with the balcony,
But the heat and light of those days
Can reach this far from time to time.
Your latest was from Senegal,
Mine from Helsinki. I don't know
If we'll meet again. Be happy.
If you hear this, send a postcard.

Sonnet of '68

by Harry Oberländer

The uproar's over, and the calls to fight
For freedom, the Utopian fantasies.
We took a fairground ride to Paradise
And afterwards there's nothing more, goodnight.

The fire burnt out. The veterans, turning grey,
Make legends of the beautiful, wild past.
These will stay with us till we breathe our last:
The red flag and the photograph of Che.

So many speeches. There's a silence now.
Each of us walks along the city street
Alone, concerned about his daily bread.

We overreached ourselves a little bit.
Euphoria didn't suit us anyhow.
Those who did not outgrow it – they are dead.

Translated from the German by the author and Wendy Cope.

A Word before Sleep

after Marina Tsvetayeva

Life tells us lies, inimitably,
Beyond all expectations, outdoing other liars.
You know, when all your veins are trembling,
You recognise it – life!

It is as if you're lying in a field of rye,
In ringing blueness, falling heat (and so what if it's lies
You're lying in), the sound of bees through honeysuckle.
Rejoice. You have been called.

No, don't reproach me, my dear friend –
Our souls are easily bewitched,
Already, now, my head is entering a dream.
Why did you sing?

Your quietnesses are a clean, white book,
Your 'yesses', savage clay.
I bend my head towards them, quietly.
The palm of my hand – life.

Tsvetayeva composed her poem in June 1922 after reading Boris Pasternak's book *My Sister Life*. I made use of a literal translation from the Russian by Gerard Smith.

After Prague

about Marina Tsvetayeva

He went. You said
you didn't want to live –

but there were other cities,
sixteen years,

before you reached the end,
alone in Yelabuga.

Hope is a long leash,
drawn in slowly.

The Sitter

Vanessa Bell, Nude, c.1922–3, *Tate Britain*

Depressed and disagreeable and fat –
That's how she saw me. It was all she saw.
Around her, yes, I may have looked like that.
She hardly spoke. She thought I was a bore.
Beneath her gaze I couldn't help but slouch.
She made me feel ashamed. My face went red.
I'd rather have been posing on a couch
For some old rake who wanted me in bed.
Some people made me smile, they made me shine,
They made me beautiful. But they're all gone,
Those friends, the way they saw this face of mine,
And her contempt for me is what lives on.
Admired, well-bred, artistic Mrs Bell,
I hope you're looking hideous in Hell.

Les Vacances

Walter Richard Sickert, Bathers, Dieppe, *1902,*
Walker Art Gallery, Liverpool

Maman et Papa au bord de la mer.
Aujourd'hui il fait beau. I remember it well.
Voilà Armand, in the corner down there,
With Maman et Papa au bord de la mer!
Oh, bored, c'est le mot. I tear out the hair
As we limp through ce livre avec Mademoiselle.
Maman et Papa au bord de la mer.
Il fait beau. I remember it only too well.

Dead Sheep Poem

This morning we saw sheepskin rugs
Outside the craft shop in the village.

Now we've found one on the hillside,
Soft and creamy-white among the thistles,

Cushioning a ribcage and a line
Of vertebrae, laid out like stepping-stones.

Nine feet away, the skull
And jawbone, clean as carved ivory.

Crows and maggots cleared off long ago –
The person with the notebook has arrived.

The Lyric Poet

from a line by Heine

```
I     ache
I           die
I   m             in
          he    l    l
I   ma      k e
        a       l ine
      ma  d
                i   l    l
        a
          ch  i  l        d
                      in
                        ne   ed
I   ma      k e
        a       l ine
          he
c     a         l     l ed
      m   e
          he
          he    l        d
      m   e
          he
                l i e    d
I   ma      k e
        a       l ine
        a           n
      ac  e     l ine
          che       e          r
```

Ich mache die kleinen Lieder

A Mystery

People say, 'What are you doing these days? What are
  you working on?'
I think for a moment or two.

The question interests me. What am I doing these days?
How odd that I haven't a clue.

Right now, of course, I'm working on this poem,
With just a few more lines to go.

But tomorrow someone will ask me, 'What are you up
  to these days? What are you working on?'
And I still won't know.

Reading Berryman's Dream Songs
at the Writers' Retreat

Wendy went a-swimming. It was dreadful.
One small boy careless under her did surface
and did butt her on the chin.
Of space to swim was hardly any,
fearful shoutings, bodies from the springboard
splash when jumping in.

Why no school? cried agey Wendy
to herself, not loud. Why little beggars
swimming into me on Friday afternoon?
Why not in cage, learn tables?
Out and dress and buy bananas.
Yogurt? No. Need spoon.

Once more to Hawthornden through Scottish fog.
Back up to poet's lair and sit on bed.
Is you bored, Bones, all by youzeself
wif read and write and bein' deep?
Not for a moment.
Now, a little sleep.

The Squirrel and the Crow

Each day I take a morning walk
Above the River Esk,
In preparation for long hours
Of writing at my desk.

And when the healthy Scottish air
Has cleared my sleepy head,
I climb three flights of stairs, collapse
Exhausted on my bed,

Pick up the daily paper, try
To solve some crossword clues,
And when I can't do any more,
Find notebook, summon Muse.

But she will not co-operate,
That wayward Muse of mine.
She seems to mutter, 'Have a heart,
It's only ten past nine.'

Though other writers all around
Type, type and do not shirk,
This maxim saves me from depression:
Reading books is work.

I pick up Edward Thomas,
Collected, fairly slim,
And read it for an hour and wish
That I could write like him.

Next day I walk with glasses on
To see what I can find
Of natural things that may, perhaps,
Improve my urban mind.

I notice tiny bugle flowers,
Each one a bright blue star
(Although, until I look them up,
I don't know what they are).

Red campion, pink purslane – riches
Everywhere I look.
Wood-sorrel, greater stitchwort (all
Are in the Oxford Book).

I wander on until I see
Before me on the track –
This will be something horrible – two lumps,
one grey, one black.

And, drawing closer, find a squirrel
Who has lost his head
Or hers. The other is a crow,
And this, too, is stone dead.

What happened? Here's my first attempt
At answering the question:
The crow bit off the squirrel's head
And died of indigestion.

I leave a note for Roy next door
(We aren't allowed to talk
Till dinner-time) and head it HORROR
ON THE CASTLE WALK!

And he, a trained zoologist,
Explains it was not so:
A squirrel is too big to be
Beheaded by a crow.

Post-mortem on the squirrel: Roy
Concludes that someone shot it.
As for the crow, we do not know
What quirk of fortune got it.

The absence of the squirrel's head
Remains a mystery.
My quiet, lovely nature poem –
That was not to be.

Men in prison: one sees stars,
Another, only mud.
Poets walking: some find solace,
Others, guts and blood.

John Clare

John Clare, I cried last night
For you – your grass-green coat,
Your oddness, others' spite,
Your fame, enjoyed and lost,
Your gift, and what it cost.

Awake in the early hours,
I heard you with my eyes,
Carolling woods and showers.
As if a songbird's throat
Could utter words, you wrote.

I listened late and long –
Each clear, true, loving note
Placed justly in its song.
Sometimes for sheer delight,
John Clare, I cried last night.

An Ending

Don't want to leave this place,
This time, this happiness:
Loud water, muddy tracks,
Trees rooted in pink rocks,
Our lush, steep-sided glen,
Friends I may see again
But certainly not here,
Not in this world we were.

For one short month our home,
This world will soon be gone.
Though those unruly birds
Still chirp and caw, though woods
Breathe on, if we return,
Each one of us alone,
It will not be to find
What we now leave behind.

Out there beyond the gates,
We'll take our random routes
Through time and space. How far,
How long, we can't be sure.
We'll have to say goodbye
To more than this one day.
Tomorrow, we rehearse,
And quietly leave this place.

Poem from a Colour Chart of House Paints

Limeglow of leaves –
elf, sapling
in Elysian green,
she's jitterbugging
in the forest.
She is froth, the tang
of julep, capering
among the ferns.

Passion, the firedance
of her fantasy,
fireglow of poppy
and corona, ember.
Casanova, peerless
demon, jester!
She burns, a firefly,
Apollo's geisha.

Her sandgold hair,
spun-silk kimono,
melon and lemon sorbet
on the balcony,
white wine, gardenias.
That honeysuckle year –
if he could ransom
one sunlit day!

Indigo seascape –
Melissa in cool,
blue moonshade.
Harebell, naiad,

exotic ballerina,
she commands the bay,
the midnight swell,
the surf, pale gossamer.

Autumnal in brogues,
beige twinset, russet
tweeds, she takes
coffee at eleven,
sherry at noon –
dreams of Tarragona,
castanets, a man
who called her Sheba.

Her mood
is violet, nocturnal.
Aubrietia, phlox,
wisteria delight her
more than roses.
Solitude, a purple
robe, a last
long hazy evening.

Greek Island Triolets

1 ENTOMOLOGICAL

This fly believes I'm dead.
I cannot lift a finger.
He buzzes round my head.
This fly believes I'm dead –
A body on a bed,
Safe place for him to linger.
This fly believes I'm dead.
I cannot lift a finger.

2 SARTORIAL

Why did I buy this Marks and Spencer's T-shirt
And, having done so, fail to take it back?
An average English-frump-beside-the-sea-shirt –
Why did I buy this Marks and Spencer's T-shirt?
I needed something ace. This is a B-shirt,
Fit only to be worn beneath a mac.
Why did I buy this Marks and Spencer's T-shirt?
Shall I wash it once and take it back?

3 ARBOREAL

We hugged a tree last night
And all of us enjoyed it.
Ecstatic, by moonlight,
We hugged a tree last night.
Trees can't put up a fight –
That oak could not avoid it.
We hugged it good and tight –
I hope the tree enjoyed it.

The Ted Williams Villanelle

for Ari Badaines

'Don't let anybody mess with your swing.'
— TED WILLIAMS, baseball player

Watch the ball and do your thing.
This is the moment. Here's your chance.
Don't let anybody mess with your swing.

It's time to shine. You're in the ring.
Step forward, adopt a winning stance,
Watch the ball and do your thing,

And while that ball is taking wing,
Run, without a backward glance.
Don't let anybody mess with your swing.

Don't let envious bastards bring
You down. Ignore the sneers, the can'ts.
Watch the ball and do your thing.

Sing out, if you want to sing.
Jump up, when you long to dance.
Don't let anybody mess with your swing.

Enjoy your talents. Have your fling.
The seasons change. The years advance.
Watch the ball and do your thing,
And don't let anybody mess with your swing.

He Tells Her

for Ruth B.

He tells her that the Earth is flat –
He knows the facts, and that is that.
In altercations fierce and long
She tries her best to prove him wrong.
But he has learned to argue well.
He calls her arguments unsound
And often asks her not to yell.
She cannot win. He stands his ground.

The planet goes on being round.

This poem also appears on page 325 as part of a sequence.

What I Think

All right, I'll tell you what I think.
I'll tell you more than once or twice:
You really ought to see a shrink.

Your psyche isn't in the pink,
Your home is not a paradise,
All right? I'll tell you what I think:

Though you get by, with friends and drink
And rhymed despair (our common vice),
You really ought to see a shrink.

Of course, it's scary. You won't sink.
You'll cry a lot. It's worth the price,
All right? I'll tell you what I think:

I've wasted breath, I'm wasting ink.
I'm smothering you with advice.
You really ought to see a shrink.

I want you happy, stupid gink.
I'm here for you till Hell is ice.
All right, I've told you what I think.
For God's sake, go and see a shrink.

The Sorrow of Socks

Some socks are loners –
They can't live in pairs.
On washdays they've shown us
They want to be loners.
They puzzle their owners,
They hide in dark lairs.
Some socks are loners –
They won't live in pairs.

The Stickleback Song

'Someone should see to the dead stickleback.'
– school inspector to London headteacher

A team of inspectors came round here today,
They looked at our school and pronounced it OK.
We've no need to worry, we shan't get the sack,
But someone should see to the dead stickleback.
Dead stickleback, dead stickleback,
But someone should see to the dead stickleback.

Well, we've got some gerbils, all thumping their tails,
And we've got a tankful of live water-snails,
But there's one little creature we certainly lack –
We haven't a quick or a dead stickleback.
Dead stickleback, dead stickleback,
We haven't a quick or a dead stickleback.

Oh was it a spectre the inspector saw,
The ghost of some poor classroom pet who's no more?
And will it be friendly or will it attack?
We're living in fear of the dead stickleback.
Dead stickleback, dead stickleback,
We're living in fear of the dead stickleback.

Or perhaps there's a moral to this little song:
Inspectors work hard and their hours are too long.
When they overdo it, their minds start to crack
And they begin seeing the dead stickleback.
Dead stickleback, dead stickleback,
And they begin seeing the dead stickleback.

Now all you young teachers, so eager and good,
You won't lose your wits for a few years, touch wood.
But take off as fast as a hare on the track
The day you encounter the dead stickleback.
Dead stickleback, dead stickleback,
The day you encounter the dead stickleback.

Stress

for Henry Thompson, but not about him

He would refuse to put the refuse out.
The contents of the bin would start to smell.
How could she be content? That idle lout
Would drive the tamest woman to rebel.
And, now that she's a rebel, he frequents
The pub for frequent drink-ups with a mate
Who nods a lot whenever he presents
His present life at home as far from great.
The drinking makes his conduct even worse
And she conducts herself like some poor soul
In torment. She torments her friends with verse,
Her protest poems – dreadful, on the whole.
We daren't protest. Why risk an upset when
She's so upset already? I blame men.

A Hampshire Disaster

'Shock was the emotion of most.'
– Hampshire Chronicle, 13 May 1994

When fire engulfed the headquarters
Of the Royal Winchester Golf Club
In the early hours of Wednesday morning,
Shock was the emotion of most.

But fear had been the emotion
Of some who saw the flames, and admiration
For the courage and skill of the firefighters
Was another emotion felt.

At the loss of so much history –
Cups, trophies, and honours boards –
Sadness is now the emotion
Of many Winchester golfers.

Stoical resignation was the emotion
Of the club captain, as he told the *Chronicle*:
'The next procedure will be to sort out the insurance.
Life must go on.'

A Poem on the Theme of Humour

for Gavin Ewart

'*Poems can be in any style and on any theme (except humour).*'
    – rules for the Bard of the Year competition 1994

Dear Organisers of Bard of the Year,

Suppose I were to write a completely solemn, joke-free and
    unamusing poem
And to send it in with my £3 entry fee,
And suppose the subject of that poem were humour in poetry,
Would you accept it?

There are serious things I want to say on this subject,
Such as how absolutely right you were to make that rule,
Because, if humour is allowed into a poem,
People may laugh and enjoy it,
Which gives the poet an unfair advantage.

I trust that the supervisor of the panel of judges, Dannie Abse,
('immediate past President of the Poetry Society and one of
    Britain's greatest poets'),
Will be rigorous in disqualifying any poem
That raises so much as a smile.

What a good idea to have a separate competition
Called 'Fun '94', with smaller prizes,
For those who write humorous poems!
It doesn't dilute your message to the reading public:
Real poetry is no fun at all.

A Reading

Everybody in this room is bored.
The poems drag, the voice and gestures irk.
He can't be interrupted or ignored.

Poor fools, we came here of our own accord
And some of us have paid to hear this jerk.
Everybody in the room is bored.

The silent cry goes up, 'How long, O Lord?'
But nobody will scream or go berserk.
He won't be interrupted or ignored

Or hit by eggs, or savaged by a horde
Of desperate people maddened by his work.
Everybody in the room is bored,

Except the poet. We are his reward,
Pretending to indulge his every quirk.
He won't be interrupted or ignored.

At last it's over. How we all applaud!
The poet thanks us with a modest smirk.
Everybody in the room was bored.
He wasn't interrupted or ignored.

How to Deal with the Press

She'll urge you to confide. Resist.
Be careful, courteous, and cool.
Never trust a journalist.

'We're off the record,' she'll insist.
If you believe her, you're a fool.
She'll urge you to confide. Resist.

Should you tell her who you've kissed,
You'll see it all in print, and you'll
Never trust a journalist

Again. The words are hers to twist,
And yours the risk of ridicule.
She'll urge you to confide. Resist.

'But X is nice,' the publicist
Will tell you. 'We were friends at school.'
Never trust a journalist,

Hostile, friendly, sober, pissed,
Male or female – that's the rule.
When tempted to confide, resist.
Never trust a journalist.

Traditional Prize County Pigs

1 WESSEX SADDLEBACK

A porcine aborigine,
He has no trace of foreign blood.
His ancestors were wild and free
British pigs in British mud.

He's a hardy, outdoor type,
Who's never heard of central heating.
He doesn't whine, he doesn't gripe
But, strong and silent, goes on eating.

2 OXFORDSHIRE SANDY AND BLACK

This piggy has a pedigree
That goes way back on Midlands farms.
If she could read her family tree,
She might design a coat of arms.

But she knows nothing of her line,
And lives like any other sow,
Taking care of little swine,
Imprisoned in the here and now.

3 CORNISH LOP-EARED

A fine white pig of goodly size,
He roots and gobbles from the ground
But when he tries to look around,
His lop ears droop across his eyes.

He doesn't know the world is big
And beautiful. He doesn't try
To wander. He's an easy pig,
Content to stay within his sty.

4   STAFFORDSHIRE TAMWORTH RED

If you want to go away
On a summer holiday
And take your pig, make no mistake,
A Tamworth Red's the pig to take.

A pig whose skin is very fair
Will use up all your Ambre Solaire,
And need a hat, and cause concern,
But Tamworths very seldom burn.

5   ORKNEY BOAR

If you should meet an Orkney Boar
A-roaming on an Orkney moor,
Beware. This savage little porker
May attack the English walker.

6   LINCOLNSHIRE CURLY COAT

A pig of pigs. If free to scoff,
He'll seldom leave the feeding-trough,
Expanding till he's almost static
And procreation's problematic.

And that, I guess, is why the breed
By now is very rare indeed.

7 GLOUCESTERSHIRE OLD SPOT

Walking Rorschach tests, Old Spots
Have pure white skin with inky blots
But do not show an interest
In asking what the shapes suggest.

8 BERKSHIRE PRIZE BEAUTY

Once the standard of perfection
By which other pigs were judged –
Lovely figure, great complexion
Even when her face was smudged.
Just imagine the dejection
As her rivals' owners trudged
To fatstock show and prize inspection,
Knowing she could not be budged.

9 OLD GLAMORGAN

There isn't very much to write –
I only know he's large and white.

10 DORSET GOLD TIP

In Dorset in the days of old
There lived a pig whose hide was gold –
Friendly, beautiful, and charming,
Unsuitable for modern farming.
It can't be helped. The world moves on
And all the golden pigs are gone.

Elegy for the Northern Wey

polluted by an ammonia spillage, March 1999

This is the moment:
March sunshine, trees almost bare,
everything stirring.

The birds know it too –
so loud, so full of themselves
this blissful morning.

White clouds. Tree-shadows.
The river. How clear it is,
how busy with life.

This is the moment
we can never get back to.
Look, a little frog.

Tulips

Months ago I dreamed of a tulip garden,
Planted, waited, watched for their first appearance,
Saw them bud, saw greenness give way to colours,
Just as I'd planned them.

Every day I wonder how long they'll be here.
Sad and fearing sadness as I admire them,
Knowing I must lose them, I almost wish them
Gone by tomorrow.

II

The Teacher's Tale

In London SE5 there lived a boy
Called Paul. He was his mother's pride and joy
When he was born in 1961 –
Best baby ever, Mrs Skinner's son.
He had a dad, too, living with his mum.
In this our Paul was luckier than some,
Since many dads of London SE5
Were not at home, though most were still alive.
Paul's dad, Gus Skinner, had a little shop
Where you could buy a dustbin or a mop,
An ironing board or other household stuff.
He wasn't rich but he had just enough
To keep his little family afloat
And buy his wife a decent winter coat
From time to time – not every other year
But one in four or five, since coats are dear.
On this they were agreed. They didn't fight
About finance. Both partners thought it right
To plan and budget with the greatest care.
They were respectable. They didn't swear.
They disapproved of swearing, and of spending,
Instead of saving, making do and mending.
They disapproved of wild carousing, noise,
And the behaviour of the local boys.

With attitudes and firm opinions this strict,
They frowned upon most people in the district.
And, naturally, they didn't want their boy
To grow up like the local hoi polloi.
They trained him to be quiet and obedient,
For his own sake, they said. But it's expedient

For parents who prefer an ordered life
(And such were Mr Skinner and his wife)
To keep their offspring under tight restraint
And bid them suffer this without complaint,
And punish them with violence or coldness
For any spontaneity or boldness.
The poor child must believe that he is blessed
With parents who act always for the best
And if they make him wretched, angry, sad,
This merely demonstrates that he is bad.
I don't believe grown-ups should let a child
Make all the rules or run completely wild
Or get its own way with a piercing scream –
There's little to be said for that extreme.
Undisciplined, spoiled children are a pain
And cause a lot of problems, that is plain,
Whereas a young unfortunate like Paul
Won't inconvenience anyone at all.
But when I hear the politicians' song
About the family and right and wrong
And discipline and all of that, I seethe,
Remembering kids who aren't allowed to breathe.
Family life can be a blessing: true
But don't forget the damage it can do.

When Paul was just a baby he was fed
According to the clock. His mother said
'He can't get everything he wants by crying.
It's best to learn that now. He'll soon stop trying.'
When he could talk, requests were often met
With the old saying, 'Those who ask don't get.'
He learned that wanting, asking were misguided.
He had to wait and see what she decided.
Sometimes his parents liked to give him treats –
Holidays and outings, presents, sweets –

And they expected lots of gratitude
And wouldn't tolerate a sulky mood.
'I don't like the expression on your face,
Young man,' he'd hear, if he betrayed a trace
Of anger. And, since children always need
To trust their parents, mostly he'd succeed
In burying his feelings, so he couldn't
Have negative emotions when he shouldn't.
They told him he was lucky. He suspected
That wasn't true, though he was not neglected
Or dressed in dirty clothes or underfed.
At half past ten his parents were in bed,
Not in a pub or club or bingo hall –
They didn't like that sort of thing at all.
He heard about kids who were left alone
At night when it was dark, all on their own.
His mother thought it dreadful. She was right.
Paul wouldn't want to be alone at night.
And yet he sometimes liked the sound
Of parents who were not always around.

Paul went to school when he was nearly five.
Like other children, when they first arrive,
He felt quite scared, but thought it best his fears
Should be kept hidden. Some kids were in tears
When it was time for Mum to say goodbye
But Paul had learned to act. He didn't cry.

School was a big surprise. Paul thought that you
Sat at a desk and got some work to do
But he was wrong, it seemed. They let you play
And read you different stories every day.
He liked the stories but felt some distress
At seeing other children make a mess
With powder paint. They got it everywhere –

The floor, their clothes, their faces and their hair.
Mum never let him make a mess like that –
She couldn't stand it in her tidy flat.

So many things to do. It was confusing:
Sometimes you had to choose and Paul found
    choosing
Quite difficult. He'd stand and have a look
Then go into a corner with a book.
A timid child, afraid to have a stab
At new activities, afraid to grab
The thing he wanted, he quite liked the times
When everyone sat down for finger rhymes
Or singing songs or learning ABC
From great big charts with pictures, although he
Got bored with that quite soon because he knew it
And didn't want to keep on going through it.
For Paul could learn things quickly, it turned out,
And no one had to be concerned about
His progress in the basic skills. However,
Though she could see that Paul was fairly clever,
His teacher noticed that the little lad
Was often serious, subdued and sad.
And, when she met his parents, she could see
What they were like, and that they might well be
The cause of his unhappiness. She tried
To help the quiet boy who never cried
And felt he always had to get things right.
She helped him see that now and then he might
Try something new and fail. She wouldn't mind.
He learned that he could trust her to be kind.
Some of the other boys were very tough
And naughty. Some girls, too, were pretty rough
But Mrs Moore (that was her name) knew how
To have them understand what she'd allow

And what would make her very, very cross.
They liked her but they knew that she was boss.

On open evening both Paul's parents sat
With Mrs Moore and had a long, long chat.
The teacher had a lot of time to spare
Because there weren't that many parents there.
Some didn't care and many were afraid
Because they felt they hadn't made the grade
At school, and, if their children were the same,
They thought they'd be told off. The Skinners came
To everything. Good parents. Lucky lad.
They'd give him hell if his report was bad
In any way at all. 'He's doing well,'
Said Mrs Moore. 'He's come out of his shell
A lot this year, and made good progress, too,
In all the basic skills. No need for you
To worry. And he's learning to have fun,'
She added. Now, that comment on her son
Did not please Mother. She was never sure
About her Paul's beloved Mrs Moore.
Her clothes were slightly odd and not the sort
A teacher ought to wear, the parent thought –
Too 'trendy' for a woman of her age.
That dreaded adjective was all the rage
And summed up everything the Skinners hated.
'Well, having fun won't get him educated.'
Mrs Moore breathed in. She mustn't get
Into an argument she might regret.
It wouldn't help the boy. She smiled her best.
'His reading and his maths and all the rest
Are excellent. And I am always glad
When pupils tell me that their mum and dad
Have bought them books.' She went on in this vein
A little while. She wished she could explain

All her beliefs about what children need.
She longed to take the couple's hands and plead
With them to be more loving, less severe
But it would do no good. That much was clear.

Perhaps I am too hard on Mum and Dad,
Presenting them as if they're wholly bad.
Some people liked them. Gus would share a joke
With customers and chat with older folk
Whose visit to his shop was all that they
Would have of human company that day.
Left to himself, the father might have been
Less harsh and strict with Paul, and not so keen
To make him an obedient marionette
But he was busy and he mostly let
His other half do things her way. And she,
What can I say? Well, Mrs S. could be
Extremely helpful if someone was ill.
She'd do their shopping, even pay the bill,
If it was small, and have their children round.
The children didn't like this much. They found
They weren't allowed to move. 'Sit there and draw
And don't drop anything on my clean floor.'
Oh dear. So much for trying to be nice
About this character. It must suffice.

Paul moved on up the school, while Mrs Moore
Stayed with the first-year infants, as before.
Though he was sad at leaving her behind,
Some years he had a teacher just as kind
But other years the teacher didn't take
To Paul, since he or she was too opaque
To grasp that being nicely dressed and clean
With interested parents doesn't mean
That everything is easy for a child.

Paul irritated them – so meek and mild,
When they liked kids with spirit. Or they thought
That he was privileged and that they ought
To take care of the disadvantaged kids,
Whose families had really hit the skids,
With dads in prison, dead or gone away,
And mums who had to struggle through each day.
Don't get me wrong. Those children needed all
The help that they could get. But so did Paul.

At ten he was a boy of average height.
Brown hair. Pale face. His build: it wasn't slight
But fairly sturdy, getting on for podgy –
The food he liked was comforting and stodgy.
By now his academic reputation
Was 'Good ability, poor concentration.'
Instead of getting on with things, he'd gaze
Out of the classroom window, in a daze,
Daydreaming, worrying or feeling sad –
He was an insecure and anxious lad.
When he made friends, his mother didn't like them.
When he had plans, she did her best to spike them.
She didn't want him going out to play
When he'd been working hard at school all day.
She wished they'd give him homework. That would keep
Him occupied until he went to sleep
And make life easier for Dad and Mum.
She sometimes went to school and asked for some.
One teacher fell in line but most refused
And Mrs Skinner wasn't much amused
When Mr Browning said, 'A boy Paul's age
Should have a social life. He's at a stage
When getting on with other boys is bound
To be important to him, and I've found

That schoolwork suffers when a child feels lonely.
I understand your fears and worries, only
I think that, if you'd let him out to play
A little more, the strategy would pay.'
'I'll have to think about it, Mr Browning,'
She said, stood up, and left the classroom, frowning.
Mr Browning didn't think this speech
Would make much difference but his words did reach
Paul's ears, by chance, because he overheard
His mother when she had a quiet word
With Dad about the teacher's point of view.
Young Paul was touched and grateful. Browning knew
And understood, it seemed. He almost cried
To think that there was someone on his side.

This Mr Browning, known to Paul as Sir,
Taught fourth-year juniors, those who would transfer
To secondary school next year. At first
He terrified the good kids – and the worst
Restrained themselves as best they could because
They'd heard tall tales about how strict he was.
And he was big – broad shoulders, six feet tall,
And very keen on football, unlike Paul,
But he was OK, Browning, it turned out –
Not every sportsman is a boorish lout.

'Wake up, Paul.' 'Sorry, Sir.' 'Be quiet, Keith.'
He kept them well and truly underneath
His ample thumb but did it with affection.
He liked them all, they knew it, and correction –
'Sit down, Michelle' – was taken in good part.
Once, when the dinner break was due to start,
He kept Paul back. 'A word.' 'Yes, Sir.' He stood
A little nervously. The brotherhood
And all the sisters left the room. Some smiled

And gave a friendly thumbs up as they filed
Past Paul. What had he done? 'It's not a moan,'
Said Mr Browning when they were alone.
'It's not a telling-off. It seems to me
That you've been working harder recently.
Would you agree?' 'I think so. Sir. Er . . . yup.'
'And I can see the difference. Keep it up.
Now listen very carefully to what
I'm just about to say, and please do not
Let it go floating out your other ear.
I want you to remember it next year
And after that. OK? You're very bright
And very likeable. Now hold on tight
To that because it's true. Don't let it go.
Your life is sometimes difficult, I know.'
Paul didn't know quite what to say. He stared
Down at his feet because he hardly dared
To look at Mr Browning, just in case
The tears began to trickle down his face.
He mumbled 'Thank you, Sir'. 'And, by the way,'
The teacher added. 'Careful what you say
To all the others. Smashing bunch of clients –
But they are not all intellectual giants.'
Paul grinned. 'Now, off you go and have your dinner.
And you remember what I said, Paul Skinner.'

The weeks flew past and soon it was July
When all the fourth years had to say goodbye
To Bridge Street School. The comprehensive
    beckoned –
The daunting Queen Elizabeth the Second –
And most of them were feeling pretty scared
Although not everybody was prepared
To say so. Paul felt lonely and bereft
When he had said his last farewells and left.

He spent the summer lying on his bed
And lost count of the library books he read.
He listened to the radio a bit
But kept the volume very low, lest it
Upset his mother – music with a beat
Affronted her – and had too much to eat.
She wasn't satisfied. 'Paul, any fool
Can read a book,' she said one day. 'And you'll
Get fat and lazy lying there like that.'
He felt like screaming. 'Come and have a chat.'
'No thanks, Mum. Not just now.' *Leave me alone.*
At least let me be quiet on my own.
He couldn't leave the flat without permission.
On his return he faced an inquisition.
She sensed that when he read a book he stole
Into a world beyond her strict control.

One thing they had to do before term started
Was buy his uniform. He trailed, downhearted,
With mother to the shops. She bought him stuff
That looked ridiculous. 'It's big enough
To last a year or two.' He begged. 'Mum, please!
People will laugh at me if I wear these.'
What did she care? 'You don't appreciate
The things I do for you, young man.' 'Yeah. Great,'
Paul muttered darkly. 'What was that you said?'
'Nothing.' He closed his eyes and shook his head.

The dreaded day arrived and Paul got dressed
In his new clothes. His mother was impressed.
'You do look smart, dear.' Then she turned to Gus.
'On this first day I think that one of us
Should walk with him to school.' 'Oh, no, Mum. No!'
Her husband acquiesced. 'All right. I'll go.'
They walked together, but not very far.

Gus stopped and said, 'OK, son. Right you are.
I think you know the way to school from here.
Good luck. And not a word to Mum.' 'No fear.
Thanks, Dad. I'll see you later.' Off he ran –
A big boy now, a frightened little man.

Enormous concrete building. Lots of noise.
Long corridors aloud with girls and boys.
Big Bridge Street fourth years now looked small
   and sweet
In their new uniforms, all clean and neat,
And on their best behaviour. Even so,
Dawn Green and her friend Michelle had a go
About Paul's clothes. 'You ever seen a clown?'
'Watch out. I think his trousers might fall down.'
They giggled. All his fears were coming true.
Please open, ground, so I can fall right through.
But then he saw some more familiar faces
Milling round the desks and finding places
And some said 'Wotcha, Paul' and some said 'Hi'
And Keith said 'Sit here, mate,' and, by and by,
He felt a little better. That first day
The pupils had to learn to find their way
From class to class and Paul got very worried,
More so than most when, late and lost, he hurried
Down corridors, round corners, up more stairs
And into wrong rooms, where he met the stares
Of lots of people who did not expect him
And vanished, so they couldn't redirect him.
Next day was not much better, nor the next.
The newest boys and girls were still perplexed
By labyrinths of endless corridors
And finding different rooms on different floors.
Some, when they knew the way, pretended not to.
They turned up late and, asked where they had got to,

Said, 'We was lost.' What could the teacher do?
At this stage in the term it could be true.

One Tuesday, on his way to drama, Paul
Bumped into Keith and Wayne outside the Hall.
''Ey, Paulie, 'ere a minute.' That was Keith.
They took him to a corner underneath
A staircase, whispered 'You like drama?' 'No.'
He hated it. He didn't want to go.
You had to throw yourself around and yell,
Express your feelings. Paul did not do well.
'Be late with us. It's OK. It's a laugh.
You'll only have to do the second half.'

They liked him, Keith and Wayne. He'd noticed that
In Mr Browning's class. They'd stop and chat
And have a laugh with him and call him 'Mate'.
Sometimes he made them laugh, and that was great.
But this was different. Paul felt pretty scared.
Bunk off part of drama? If he dared,
He wouldn't have to roll around the floor
Or stretch his arms and stamp his feet and roar,
Or not for forty minutes, anyway.
And he liked Wayne and Keith. Why not? 'OK.'
'Right. Follow me. This way,' said Keith. 'Stay cool.'
He sauntered confidently through the school
And through a door, across the playground to
The outdoor toilets. Paul was in a stew
Already, filled with terror and regret.
Keith calmly offered him a cigarette.
Paul shook his head. 'No thanks.' *Oh God*, he
    thought,
We're in dead trouble now, if we get caught.
Keith lit up, closed his eyes as he inhaled.
Wayne tried to look as cool as him but failed

And had a coughing fit. 'Hold this for me
A minute, Paul. I got to have a pee.'
Paul took it. Suddenly he froze with fear.
Footsteps. An adult voice. 'Right. Out of here.'
Mr Smart, schoolkeeper on the prowl,
Was standing in the doorway with a scowl.
'Put out those fags. Don't leave them on the floor.
I'll take the rest, if you've got any more.'
The upshot of this serious transgression:
They had to go and make a full confession
To Mr Yates, the deputy, who tore
A strip or two off them and furthermore
Condemned them to detention. 'Four till five
Tomorrow. And make sure that you arrive.'

Paul had to tell his mother. Hell to pay.
She wouldn't speak when he got home next day.
Cold anger for a week. To Paul it seemed
As if she hated him. Some mothers screamed
And yelled at you. His mother's martyred face
And hostile silence kept him in disgrace.
'I'm sorry Mum. I won't skip class again.'
He tried apologising now and then.
It made no difference with Mum or Dad.
'Your mother's disappointed in you, lad,
And so am I.' He waited for the thaw
But he was never quite forgiven for
His escapade or, rather, for the fact
That he had the capacity to act
As if he were a separate human being,
Without his mother knowing or agreeing.

Did things improve as months and years went by?
Did Mrs Skinner change? And did pigs fly?
Paul sulked at home and learned to play the fool

With Wayne and Keith and other boys at school.
He might as well, since nothing but perfection
Would win him Mum's approval and affection.

She tried to crush his spirit but she failed –
The anger and the life in him prevailed.
He was a mixed-up kid – that's no surprise,
A thorough nuisance, in most teachers' eyes,
A silly boy who liked to mess about,
Intelligent – of that there was no doubt,
But not inclined to work. His concentration
Was pretty poor, likewise his motivation.
As for the parents – all the teaching staff
Knew Skinner had a mother-and-a-half
Who fussed, complained and gave them much advice
On how to do their jobs. She wasn't nice
To deal with. Parents do not always see
That treating teachers with hostility
Will never ever help their darling child,
But cause the family to be reviled
And laughed at in the staffroom. Mrs S.
Became a joke, a monster. As you'll guess,
This made some teachers harder on young Paul.
The prejudice did not affect them all
But he had lots of different teachers here,
Yes, nine or ten, and some changed every year.
The nice ones didn't really get to know him
And Wayne and Keith were always there to show him
That comic business or a muttered quip
Could win you warmth, affection, fellowship.
Paul needed that. His friends were all he had.
He couldn't think of Wayne and Keith as bad.

So, when they said it was OK to nick
A few sweets from the shop, or deftly pick

A magazine or two and stuff them under
Your shirt or sweater, he began to wonder.
Now he was old enough to question all
The values Mum and Dad had taught their Paul.
*A boy must be obedient, clean and quiet
And never answer back.* Paul didn't buy it.
*A boy must share his parents' narrow creed
For they are always right.* Paul disagreed,
And he was good and ready to rebel,
Throw out bathwater and the babe as well.
Perhaps it isn't always wrong to take
What isn't yours. 'What difference does it make?
Shopkeepers do all right. They make a profit
And we just knock a small percentage off it.'
Well, that was Keith's view, frequently expressed.
Paul listened, and, at first, he was distressed
But he got used to it. A year or so
Went by before he thought he'd have a go
And, when he did, it wasn't so much greed
As anger that impelled him to the deed.

His mother, every time she was annoyed
By anything he said or did, enjoyed
Announcing that he'd forfeited – again –
His pocket money for the week, and then
She'd add, 'Remember: he who pays the piper
May call the tune.' *You cow*, he thought. *You viper.*
The scene, repeated nearly every week,
Made Paul so furious he dared not speak.
He'd mutter, as he lay awake at night,
'If I become a thief, it serves her right.'

At last, one day, while mooching round a shop,
He reached out for a penny lollipop
And put it in his pocket. No one saw.

Paul Skinner on the wrong side of the law!
Next day a bar of chocolate was his swag,
And then a tin of cola in his bag,
Some nice new pencils. These he showed with pride
To Wayne and Keith, who saw the funny side.
'You nicked them?' 'Yup.' 'Now, Paul, that's very
    wrong,'
Admonished Keith. All three laughed loud and long,
And, for a moment, Paul was close to joy –
He felt as if he was a normal boy.

For several months he got away with it
But he became less careful, bit by bit.
One morning, as he helped himself to tuck,
Inevitably, retribution struck.
The shopkeeper was watching. Paul walked out.
As soon as he had left, he heard a shout,
'Hey you!' He panicked. Should he run or bluff?
He scarpered but he wasn't fast enough.

Back to the shop. The police. To Carter Street,
The local nick, where he would have to meet
His outraged parents. Now that all was lost,
Paul felt entirely calm, as if a frost
Had numbed him, and his head was very clear.
It's happened. There is nothing left to fear.
Cold anger made him brave. *When they arrive,
I'll just stay calm and quiet. I'll survive.
And what comes after that won't be as bad –
I'd rather face a court than Mum and Dad.*

And then a memory came into his head
That made this waiting-time a watershed.
Some words came back to him: 'You're very bright
And very likeable. Now hold on tight

To that because it's true. Don't let it go.
Your life is sometimes difficult, I know.'
And suddenly he had to fight back tears.
He sat and thought about the Bridge Street years
When he was small and promising and good,
How Mr Browning saw and understood
What he was up against. And Mrs Moore –
She'd liked him, too, when he was only four.
If they knew what was happening to me,
How sad and disappointed they would be.
Recalling all their warmth and kindness now,
Paul saw himself through their eyes, and saw how
His life was going wrong. Yes, he'd been clever.
You wouldn't think so now because he never
Did any work. He only messed about.
He'd gone on stealing till he got found out.
He could go on like this, just wasting time
And drift into a life of petty crime
To spite his parents and to demonstrate
That they were not the masters of his fate.
Would changing now mean he had given in?
Perhaps there was a better way to win.

At last the dreaded moment. Here they were –
Two policemen, followed by his dad and her,
Red-eyed and yet majestic, every inch
The martyred matriarch. Paul didn't flinch
Or hang his head like someone in disgrace,
But sat up straight and looked her in the face.

Throughout the interview, he was polite.
He told the truth. His manner was contrite
When he was speaking to the police. If Mum
Said anything, he acted deaf and dumb.
He got off with a caution – just fourteen,

A first offender, and a boy who'd been
Brought up by decent, law-abiding folk
And didn't think that all this was a joke.
Paul listened to the caution gravely, then
Vowed silently he'd never steal again.

Back home, it was the silent treatment. Paul
Stayed in his room, not staring at the wall
But working as he'd never worked before.
Next day, he was escorted door to door
By both his parents. When they reached the school,
Heads turned. Paul was aware he looked a fool
But what the hell. He wouldn't let those two
Get in the way of what he had to do.

''Ey, Paul! What 'appened?' News of his arrest
Had reached his mates, and they were both impressed
And sympathetic. Paul told them the story
Although he didn't want the kind of glory
That being nicked could bring. Not now. But they
Were still his friends. He added, 'By the way,
I've done some thinking.' 'Did it 'urt your 'ead?'
'I'm going to try and work at school,' Paul said.
Wayne laughed. Keith nodded. 'Not a bad idea,
If you don't die of boredom by next year.'
'Yeah, well, it's risky,' Paul agreed. 'We'll see.'
All day he listened hard – in geography,
In French, in maths, and he felt pretty good
When school was over, till he saw what stood
And waited for him with a face like stone.
Then he remembered, with an inward groan,
What he still had to go through. 'Hello, Mum,'
He said politely. 'Nice of you to come.'
'If I were you, young man, I wouldn't dare
To be sarcastic. I'd be too aware

Of all the hurt and trouble I had caused,
And I would hang my head in shame.' She paused
And looked disdainfully and hard at Paul,
Who didn't hang his head, but stood up tall
And walked beside her looking neither sad
Nor happy. 'I've been talking with your dad
And, when he gets home we'll be telling you
What we've decided that we have to do.'

Early that evening the parental team
Outlined their errant offspring's new regime:
No going out alone, no cash to spend –
A stricter house arrest. When would it end?
They didn't say. All much as Paul expected.
He was determined not to look dejected
But listened quietly, his face a mask,
Which egged his angry mother on to ask
'What have you got to say? We haven't yet
Heard anything from you about regret.
You sit there like a dummy. What did we
Do to deserve this, Paul? Can you tell me?'
I could but it won't help. 'Say something, Paul.'
'I'll never break the law again. That's all.'
'And no apology?' Paul sat there, dumb.
I've got an iron curtain round me, Mum
And I don't owe you anything. I'm free
To see things in my own way, to be me.

When Paul was older, he would sometimes cry
To think of that fourteen-year-old. And I
Am almost crying as I picture him
Alone, now, in his room, and know how grim
The next few years will be. He worked at school,
While all around him others played the fool.
It wasn't easy. Wayne and Keith were irked –

Attempting to distract him while he worked,
They couldn't. 'Paul would rather do a graph,'
Said Keith to Wayne one day, 'than have a laugh.'
They fell about. 'That's good. Perhaps you'll be
A poet, Keith.' 'Oh, no. No thanks. Not me.'
Some of the teachers, on the other hand,
Were slow to notice or to understand
The change in Paul. He'd been 'a waste of space',
'A tiresome idiot', 'a hopeless case'
Since entering the school. But others saw
That he was trying harder than before
And gave him the encouragement he needed
And did their best to see that he succeeded
In passing some exams. And all this time,
Paul's quiet self-containment was a crime
In Mother's eyes. He'd slipped from her control.
He had a sense of purpose and a goal
But it was his, not hers. He didn't care
If she approved or not. He wasn't there,
Not really. Now and then she'd have a go
At getting through. He didn't want to know,
Though sometimes he would have a chat with Dad
When she was out. It always made him sad.
It made him long for happy family life –
If only Gus had had a different wife.
But then, of course, Paul wouldn't have been Paul
But someone else, if he'd been born at all.

When he reached sixteen Paul was old enough
To leave both home and school. Those years were tough.
An office job, a bedsit, evening classes,
Eventually enough A level passes
To get to college. Sometimes in the night
He had to tell himself, 'You're very bright,'

And when he felt depressed and all alone
The thought of all the people he had known
Who'd liked him, kept him going, helped him find
Some thoughtful, understanding friends, the kind
He needed. Even so, he'd sometimes sink
Into depression – had to see a shrink
For quite a while. That helped. But Paul can see
That life, for him, is never going to be
A piece of cake. He teaches nowadays.
He isn't bad at it. In certain ways
He's very good, especially – you'll have guessed –
With troubled children who have been oppressed
At home. Paul lives alone. He isn't gay.
I think he'll find someone to love one day
Not too far off – it's not for me to rush him.
I hope that his exhausting job won't crush him.
I wish him health and happiness and all
The best that life can bring. God bless you, Paul.

UNCOLLECTED POEMS

— 1992–2000 —

At Cathedral Mattins

I greet them with a friendly smile.
They look at me as if I'm odd –
The haves of Hampshire, congregating
In the house of God.

Cathedral Limerick

The choir sings 'Grant us thy salvay-see-oan'
And I am assailed by temptay-see-oan –
Seized by the idea
For this limerick, I fear.
Lord, grant me improved concentray-see-oan.

Mozart in the Shopping Centre

Three scruffy teenagers
Are playing Mozart in the Brooks
So beautifully that shoppers turn their backs
On Argos, MVC and Waterstones
To stand and listen as the strings
Sing out pure happiness.

There's quite a crowd of us.
I may not be the only one
To blink back tears. It isn't just the music
But the people, sharing this,
Who came out shopping on a rainy Saturday
And chanced on the sublime.

Autumn Haiku

Leaves. Leaves everywhere:
in the garden, in the house.
Husband, wipe your feet.

Poem for L

Despite the piles of books and papers
on the kitchen table, and the ashtrays
and the worrying about your smoking and your drinking
and your weight, in spite of your annoyance
when I tell you there's a food mark on your tie,
in spite of your opinions and the way
you make them sound like facts, in spite
of your attempts to hog the newspaper
by sitting with your elbows on a pile of them,
in spite of how you read them in the bath
and make them wet, in spite of knowing
that it isn't, any of it, going to change,
you can be sure I'll still be here when you come back
because I love you more than anything
and I am stuck with it, and that is that.

Egg Cookery

An omelette doesn't want stirring –
It turns into scrambled eggs.
Forgive me, please, for demurring.
An omelette doesn't want stirring.
Dad knows. He isn't deferring
To us, although everyone begs:
An omelette doesn't want stirring!
He's done it. We've got scrambled eggs.

Riddle

A three-letter word beginning with f
And rhyming with bumblebee.
I've just read your letter, keen-eyed as a ref,
And that three-letter word beginning with f
Appears to be missing. Dear Sir, I am deaf
To your earnest and eloquent plea.
Try a three-letter word beginning with f.
Make it fat, like a bumblebee.

The South Bank Poetry Library, London

This is a pleasant library. I'd enjoy every minute
But for the danger of meeting other poets in it.

Team Spirit

Oh no, not him, sir. He's no good.
I didn't ask to join their team.
I try, but I run out of steam
And let them down again. Dead wood.

The joys of sporting brotherhood
Are not for me. I spoil their scheme.
Oh no, not him, sir. He's no good.
I didn't ask to join their team.

How many afternoons I've stood
And heard the PE master scream
What's up, lad? Are you in a dream?

I wish I was. I wish I could.
But this is real and I'm no good
And hell is being in a team.

Pianists

Now, children, this fine animal is called the pianist,
One day he may delight us all with Chopin or with Liszt,

Perhaps. But there's a price to pay. Sometimes he feels quite sad
As he regales our ears with scales, knowing it drives us mad.

Look, two of them! Keep very quiet. They are concentrating.
The pianist doesn't bite but interruptions are frustrating.

Can you give them sugar lumps? No, children, I think not.
Just wait until you're sure they've finished, then applaud a lot.

They'll bow and smile and smile and bow, and if you shout
    'Encore!'
We'll have to stay a little longer, while they play some more.

Commissioned by the Apollo Chamber Orchestra for a performance of *Carnival of the Animals* by Saint-Saëns.

Strugnell's Royal Wedding Poem

Where art thou Muse? Phone home. I need you here.
Inspire me. Help me call on all my skill
To celebrate the wedding of the year
And show I'm People's Poet of Tulse Hill.
I wouldn't want a royal prince's life –
You can't go down the pub with all your mates.
I'm glad he's found a smart and sexy wife
To keep him company behind the gates.
And, after what *The Sun* did to the bride
(Rushed out and bought it, shouldn't be allowed)
I'd like to let them know I'm on their side
And voice the feelings of the silent crowd.
Here's to you both. I hope you like my rhyme.
(I will accept a knighthood any time.)

Commissioned by a newspaper for Prince Edward's wedding but not published.

Thirteen Ways of Curing a Headache

Skyros Centre, 1993

1. Let me massage your head.

2. Let me massage your neck and shoulders.

3. Let me massage your ovaries.

4. What you need is reflexology.

5. Rub your palms together for half a minute. Then, when they are full of energy, place them over your eyes.

6. Describe the shape of your headache. Exaggerate it. Then change the shape in your mind, until the headache is better.

7. Just sit here and relax while I focus your energy points.

8. Just lie here while I work on your aura.

9. Drink this herbal tea. There is a lot of fire in you.

10. Drink *this* herbal tea. There is a lot of confused air in you.

11. Rub this menthol block over your forehead.

12. Stand on your head for at least three minutes.

13. Take two paracetamol.

from TWO CURES FOR LOVE

Selected Poems 1979–2006

— 2008 —

An Attempt at Unrhymed Verse

People tell you all the time,
Poems do not have to rhyme.
It's often better if they don't
And I'm determined this one won't.
                        Oh dear.

Never mind, I'll start again.
Busy, busy with my pen . . . cil.
I can do it, if I try –
Easy, peasy, pudding and gherkins.

Writing verse is so much fun,
Cheering as the summer weather,
Makes you feel alert and bright,
'Specially when you get it more or less the way
   you want it.

Limerick

A talented young chimpanzee
Was keen to appear on TV.
He wrote to Brooke Bond
But they didn't respond
So he had to become an MP.

FAMILY VALUES

— 2011 —

A Christmas Song

Why is the baby crying
On this, his special day,
When we have brought him lovely gifts
And laid them on the hay?

He's crying for the people
Who greet this day with dread
Because somebody dear to them
Is far away or dead,

For all the men and women
Whose love affairs went wrong,
Who try their best at merriment
When Christmas comes along,

For separated parents
Whose turn it is to grieve
While children hang their stockings up
Elsewhere on Christmas Eve,

For everyone whose burden,
Carried through the year,
Is heavier at Christmastime,
The season of good cheer.

That's why the baby's crying
There in the cattle stall:
He's crying for those people.
He's crying for them all.

Christmas Ornaments

The mice attacked the Holy Family –
The one I bought in Prague, made out of straw.
By Christmas, Joseph was an amputee
And Mary and the baby were no more.
But I have other treasures to display –
Two perching birds, a Santa Claus, a clown,
A rooster from the church in Santa Fe,
A little harp and drum, a shoe, a crown –
Collected in the years I've lived with you,
The years of warmth and love and Christmas trees,
And someone to come home to, someone who
Can share what I bring back from overseas
And sometimes travel with me. Darling, look –
Our moon from Paris, glittering on its hook.

Cathedral Carol Service

Those of us who are not important enough
To have places reserved for us,
And who turned up too late to get a seat at all,
Stand in the nave aisles, or perch on stone ledges.

We shiver in the draught from the west door.
We cannot see the choir, the altar or the candles.
We can barely see the words on our service sheets.

But we can hear the music. And we can sing
For the baby whose parents were not important enough
To have a place reserved for them,
And who turned up too late to get a room at all.

O Come, All Ye Faithful

Born the King of Angels –
That's the bit drives music teachers
Round the bend. 'It's An-gels.
Two notes. Not A-an-gels.'
I've fought some battles
With that extra note
And still get wound up every Christmas.

Daddy had a different problem
With the same hymn.
Sing all ye citizens
Of Heaven above.
'Heaven', he asserted,
'Is not a city.
It should be *denizens*.'

And that was what he sang.
It wasn't too embarrassing
But I can't sing the verse
Without remembering. In recent years
I have paid tribute to his memory
By singing, rather quietly,
'Denizens of Heaven above.'

Differences of Opinion

1 HE TELLS HER

He tells her that the Earth is flat –
He knows the facts, and that is that.
In altercations fierce and long
She tries her best to prove him wrong.
But he has learned to argue well.
He calls her arguments unsound
And often asks her not to yell.
She cannot win. He stands his ground.

The planet goes on being round.

2 YOUR MOTHER KNOWS

Your mother *knows* the earth's a plane
And, challenged, sheds a martyr's tear.
God give her strength to bear this pain –
A child who says the world's a sphere!

Challenged, she sheds a martyr's tear.
It's bad to make your mother cry
By telling her the world's a sphere.
It's very bad to tell a lie.

It's bad to make your mother cry.
It's bad to think your mother odd.
It's very bad to tell a lie.
All this has been ordained by God.

It's bad to think your mother odd.
The world is round. That's also true.
All this has been ordained by God.
It's hard to see what you can do.

The world is round. That *must* be true.
She's praying, hoping you will change.
It's hard to see what you can do.
Already people find you strange.

She's praying, hoping you will change.
You're difficult. You don't fit in.
Already people find you strange.
You know your anger is a sin.

You're difficult. You don't fit in.
God give her strength to bear this pain.
You know your anger is a sin.
Your mother knows the earth's a plane.

Sunday Morning

Sunday morning. Things get tense.
Will I go along
To church with Mummy or stay home,
Depressed and in the wrong?

It's a communion service
And I cannot go up,
A doubter and a sinner,
To take the silver cup.

I'll get my coat and come with you
As long as you don't mind
If, when you go up to the front,
I choose to stay behind.

But that is not acceptable.
She says it will not do.
If you don't take communion,
What will they think of you?

It's better if you stay at home,
She tells me angrily,
Which means another ruined day
For Mummy and for me.

You're Not Allowed

You're not allowed to wonder if it's true:
She loves you very much. She tells you so.
She is the one who knows what's best for you.
She tells you what to do and where to go.

She loves you very much. She tells you so.
That's why she's sending you to boarding school.
She tells you what to do and where to go
And there is no appeal against her rule.

And now she's sending you to boarding school.
She'll be upset if you are cross and sad.
And there is no appeal against this rule:
If Mummy is upset, you must be bad.

Her children often make her cross and sad
And then she cries. She cries and sulks all day.
If Mummy is upset, you must be bad.
It's no good saying sorry. You must pay.

You watch her cry. She cries and sulks all day.
You'd make your mother happy, if you could.
It's no use saying sorry. You must pay.
Things will get better, if you're very good.

You'd make your mother happy, if you could.
She is the one who knows what's best for you.
Things will get better, if you're very good.
You're not allowed to wonder if it's true.

Daily Help

in memory of Margaret Arnold 1900–91

I

You seem so small
now you are old
and I am not a child.
Your hair is yellow-white,
your eyes have paled

to the colour of the sea
on summer evenings
and the hands
that cleaned our house for years
are puffed and painful.

You don't need us now –
your children care for you;
their grandchildren
demand your company
as eagerly as we did.

Yet that huge photograph
of us remains in place.
And when I visit you
you say, 'I can't help
loving you, you know.'

Others taught us to be prudent,
thrifty, fold our serviettes –
all those important lessons.
We hug. Tears disarrange
my manners as I leave.

2

If Mrs Arnold yelled at Marian
To come and put her pyjamas away,
Marian just ran upstairs and did it.
No argument. No tears.
And she was instantly forgiven.
Mrs Arnold didn't sulk all day
If you did something wrong.

It wasn't just that she was nicer
Than Mummy. She radiated love
Like a little walking sun
And children loved her back.

We heard a lot about her grandsons,
Who were our age. Later on
I learned she'd had a daughter
Who had died in childhood
And I saw a photograph – a girl
With curly hair like mine.

When we'd moved away
She was a star turn as a dinner-lady
In her local school. But she missed us.

Before I went to boarding school
When I was seven, I asked her
To kiss my teddy bear
Because he was coming with me
And the kiss would come too.
In the darkness of the dormitory
I held his cheek to mine
And knew that Mrs Arnold
Was kissing me goodnight.

Boarders

I

Boarders are better than daygirls.
We never questioned that belief.

We were tough. We could survive
Without our mummies and our daddies,

Not like feeble daygirls.
'Feeble' was our worst insult.

Secretly I knew I was feeble
And lived in fear of being teased.

'Teasing' was our word for bullying.
The bossy girls picked out the victims,

Sometimes turning on one of their own.
Mostly it was verbal;

Now and then a cry went up,
'Chase for Trudy Tipple!'

The girl took flight. The mob
Pursued its human quarry.

I didn't join in. I like to think
It wasn't just because I couldn't run.

2

Once there was a special party:
Every boarder had to invite a daygirl.

My choice was Susan Bird,
A gentle girl. I liked her face.

I felt I was doing her an honour.
I was willing to be her friend.

But nothing came of it.
Even though I was a boarder

And she a mere daygirl,
She didn't jump at the chance.

3

I wasn't teased much. The worst time
Was in my first year

Because some older girls decided
That I used too many long words.

I soon learned not to.
Look at how I write.

Omo

One cold day, emerging
From the cloakroom,
Wrapped up in a hooded coat
And gloves and boots,
She announced 'I'm an Omo!'

When I'd stopped laughing
I told her the word was 'Eskimo'
But after that I called her 'Omo'
And it caught on. It was affectionate.
She never complained.

They called me 'Copper'
Because it was a bit like Cope.
We were a pair: Copper and Omo.
We sat together, played together,
And the bullies left us alone.

I still love Omo.
These days I use her real name
But I don't dare to mention it.
She hides from cameras. And now
I've gone and put her in a poem.

The Women's Merchant Navy

Mummy's cousin Evelyn,
Who was more like a sister to her,
Married an officer
In the Merchant Navy. Eddie Snaith.

He served on convoys
All through World War II.
Dangerous work.
His whereabouts were always secret.

He had his master's ticket.
Early in the fifties he got a ship.
A ship's captain!
I was very proud of him.

I learned that you could join
The Royal Navy, if you were a woman,
And be a Wren. I asked
About the Women's Merchant Navy.

There wasn't one,
Which seemed all wrong to me.
I decided I would found it
When I grew up.

It lasted quite a long time,
That ambition. When I was eleven
I went for an interview
At a new school.

'What do you want to do
When you grow up?'
The headmistress asked.
'Found the Women's Merchant Navy.'

She looked at my mother,
Who explained about Uncle Eddie.
I had a strong suspicion
That both of them thought it was funny.

The Africans

Visitors from Africa!
I must have been three or four
When I was told they were coming.

I knew about Africans from picture books.
They had black skin. They wore grass skirts
And beads. They danced around with spears.
I was excited and a bit scared.

When the day arrived
I stood in the back garden,
Looking through a wrought-iron gate
At the path to the front door.

And there they were, the Africans,
But they were white. Their clothes
Were just like ours.

I don't know if I hid my disappointment.
Was I good?
The rest of the day is lost.

But I can see them now,
Their many-coloured beads,
Their black skins shining,

Grass skirts rustling,
As they enter our suburban garden
And walk towards the house.

Uncle Bill

Mummy's working-class relations
Didn't get invited to dinner or tea
But Uncle Bill dropped in
From time to time, to see Nanna
Because she was his sister.
'Hello Uncle Bill,' we'd say
As he passed through the hall
On his way to the kitchen
Or Nanna's room.
He didn't stay long. When he left
We said goodbye. And that
Was all we ever saw of Uncle Bill.

Except that sometimes we'd be on a bus –
You got on at the back
And didn't see the driver –
And, even though we'd pinged to get off,
It went on past our stop
Until it reached our house.
We jumped off, my sister and I,
And ran along to the driver's cab.
'Uncle Bill! Uncle Bill!'
He waved back and drove away.

Brahms Cradle Song

I've heard it on the radio
Twice in two days –
In an item about sleep
And in *Cider with Rosie*,
When Laurie plays it on the violin,
Much too fast, like a jig.

My mother used to sing it to me
At bedtime. I liked the tune
And the words: roses,
Silvery light, God
Watching over us
Until it's time to wake up.

She read me *Black Beauty*.
She made me learn the piano.
She taught me to swim,
Despite Daddy's fear of the water,
And, after the accident
In the instructor's car, to drive.

For all that, I am grateful.
As for the rest, I can begin
To imagine forgiving her
When I am reminded
Of a young woman singing
About roses asleep in the dew.

Greydawn

We used it every day
When I was growing up.
The name stamped on the back
Is *Greydawn* – all one word.
It isn't grey. It's blue.

I made this point quite often.
'Why do they call it grey?'
The grown-ups didn't know
And tired of the question.
I still wonder.

There are three plates left –
Medium-sized, pudding plates.
All the rest – dinner and cheese plates,
Soup bowls – have disappeared,
Like the people who used them.

Mummy, Daddy, Nanna,
Sitting round the dining-room table.
And I have spun through the air
Into the future, all by myself,
With three of our blue plates.

At Stafford Services

'... places of transit where we are aware
of a particular kind of alienated poetry.'
— ALAIN DE BOTTON

In the Wimpy Bar at Stafford services
I ask for ketchup. The girl gives me a sachet.
She seems nice, so I mention the red plastic tomatoes
That used to be on every table in the old days.
She has never heard of them. She thinks
Ketchup on the tables is a good idea.

The red plastic tomatoes, the formica tables
In the Wimpy Bar by Barnehurst bus depot
Where I went, aged thirteen, to smoke,
Drink coffee and feel sophisticated.
It was all so modern, so American, so young,
And a safe haven from parents.

Fifty years on I'm sitting in another one,
Drinking coffee and not smoking.
As the light fades the glass walls turn into mirrors,
Lending the place an air of glamour. I like it here.
I could be in an Edward Hopper painting,
A woman travelling alone on business.

No one knows anything about me. Perhaps
I'm a high-powered executive with a BMW
Outside in the car park. Or some kind of artist,
A poet, maybe, scribbling in her notebook.
Dreams in a Wimpy. I finish my coffee,
Find my keys, and walk out of the picture.

At the Poetry Conference

Melancholy's grape: today I've bitten it.
I'm sad because you live so far away.
I need to write a poem but I've written it
Already: 1989, LA.

Here we are again and I am crying.
Nothing has changed except that we are old.
We will be far apart when we are dying.
One will go. The other will be told

By phone or email and it will be over.
The survivor will sit down and weep
And write a poem mourning the ex-lover
And have a drink or two and go to sleep.

That will be that. You see I'm alternating
Two kinds of rhyme, the way you recommend.
I trust you'll give these lines a Grade A rating
And that, of course, will cheer me up no end.

The Health Scare

I'm living with Uncertainty and Fear.
I need to say their names and make them rhyme.
Two monsters. I can't make them disappear.
I'm living with Uncertainty and Fear.
Though abstract nouns are not a good idea,
And abstract nouns with capitals, a crime,
I'm living with Uncertainty and Fear.
It helps to say their names and make them rhyme.

Sixty-one

Sixty-one and on a diet.
Will I end up thin or fat
When my heart and brain go quiet?
Sixty-one and on a diet
Yet again. My hopes run riot:
Better life, new start – all that.
Sixty-one and on a diet.
Will I end up thin or fat?

Keep Saying This

Keep saying this and don't forget:
Although you think you're very old,
The party isn't over yet.

You lie awake at night beset
By dread of being dead and cold.
Keep saying this and don't forget:

It doesn't help at all to fret
About what cannot be controlled.
The party isn't over yet.

Although your nature wasn't set
In a serene or fearless mould,
Keep saying this and don't forget:

In ten years time you may regret
Surrendering to gloom. Be bold.
The party isn't over yet.

No point in living if you let
Your terror of the end take hold.
Keep saying this and don't forget
The party isn't over yet.

Once I'm Dead

Once I'm dead, I won't mind being dead.
Why worry? I don't want to say goodbye
To everything, to me – the voice that said
'Once I'm dead, I won't mind being dead',
The words are comforting. But still I dread
The day that we must part, myself and I.
The voice may still be heard when I am dead
But not by me. I will have said goodbye.

My Funeral

I hope I can trust you, friends, not to use our relationship
As an excuse for an unsolicited ego-trip.
I have seen enough of them at funerals and they make
   me cross.
At this one, though deceased, I aim to be the boss.
If you are asked to talk about me for five minutes, please
   do not go on for eight.
There is a strict timetable at the crematorium and nobody
   wants to be late.
If invited to read a poem, just read the bloody poem.
   If requested
To sing a song, just sing it, as suggested,
And don't say anything. Though I will not be there,
Glancing pointedly at my watch and fixing the speaker
   with a malevolent stare,
Remember that this was how I always reacted
When I felt that anybody's speech, sermon or poetry
   reading was becoming too protracted.
Yes, I was impatient and intolerant, and not always polite
And if there aren't many people at my funeral, it will
   serve me right.

Seeing You

Seeing you will make me sad.
I want to do it anyway.
We can't relive the times we had –
Seeing you will make me sad.
Perhaps it's wrong. Perhaps it's mad,
But we will both be dead one day.
Seeing you will make me sad.
I have to do it anyway.

Macedonia 1987

A little crowd had gathered in the square.
We read our poems and they were polite.
Then there was dinner in the open air
Outside the castle. A warm summer night.
The local bigwigs lit up their cigars
And asked us for a song, and, straight away,
You stood. I see you underneath the stars.
I hear your voice. I hear it to this day.
I too can sing but I am English, so,
Although I wanted to, I didn't dare.
And still, though that was twenty years ago,
A male voice singing German takes me there.
Bach and Schubert won't let me forget
That evening, five days after we first met.

Dutch Portraits

To find myself in tears is a surprise –
Paintings don't often get to me like this:
These faces with their vulnerable eyes
And lips so soft that they invite a kiss;
The long-haired husband, gazing at his bride
With evident desire, his hand around
Her wrist, six years before she died –
Both so alive and so long underground.
And here's a husband who resembles you
When you were plump and bearded. It's too much.
He looks so happy and his wife does too,
Still smiling, now they can no longer touch.
Someone will read our story, by and by.
Perhaps they'll feel like this. Perhaps they'll cry.

Haiku

A perfect white wine
is sharp, sweet and cold as this:
birdsong in winter.

April

The birds are singing loudly overhead,
As if to celebrate the April weather.
I want to stay in this lovely world forever
And be with you, my love, and share your bed.
I don't believe I'll see you when we're dead.
I don't believe we'll meet and be together.
The birds are singing loudly overhead.
I want to stay in this lovely world forever.

The Month of May

'O! the month of May, the merry month of May...'
— THOMAS DEKKER (d. 1632)

The month of May, the merry month of May,
So long awaited, and so quickly past.
The winter's over, and it's time to play.

I saw a hundred shades of green today
And everything that Man made was outclassed.
The month of May, the merry month of May.

Now hello pink and white and farewell grey.
My spirits are no longer overcast.
The winter's over and it's time to play.

Sing 'Fa la la la la', I dare to say
(Tried being modern but it didn't last),
'The month of May, the merry month of May.'

I don't know how much longer I can stay.
The summers come, the summers go so fast,
And soon there will be no more time to play.

So *carpe diem*, gather buds, make hay.
The world is glorious. Compare, contrast
December with the merry month of May.
Now is the time, now is the time to play.

Lissadell

Last year we went to Lissadell.
The sun shone over Sligo Bay
And life was good and all was well.

The bear, the books, the dinner-bell,
An air of dignified decay.
Last year we went to Lissadell.

This year the owners had to sell –
It calls to mind a Chekhov play.
Once life was good and all was well.

The house is now an empty shell,
The contents auctioned, shipped away.
Last year we went to Lissadell

And found it magical. 'We fell
In love with it', we sometimes say
When life is good and all is well.

The light of evening. A gazelle.
It seemed unchanged since Yeats's day.
Last year we went to Lissadell
And life was good and all was well.

At Steep

We stumble down the sloping path
Clutching at trunks and branches, then
A few more steps, another tree,
Until at last we see the stone.

'That must be it.' There is no sign
On road or path to say it's there
But walkers pass this way and learn
Your name and find out who you were,

And pilgrims clutching leaflets come
From time to time, walk half a mile
To sit by your memorial
And keep you company awhile.

No. You're beyond all company.
Numbers and words inscribed on stone
Are all that's left of you where once
You felt the sun, the blessed rain.

Numbers and words inscribed on stone.
You're dead and gone and speaking still.
Your spirit lives; it brought us here.
You cannot know, and never will.

Edward Thomas lived at Steep in Hampshire. There is a memorial to him on a hillside outside the village.

A Villanelle for Hugo Williams

What can I say? I'd like to be polite
But have you ever *seen* a villanelle?
You ask me 'Have I got the rhyme-scheme right?'

Is that a joke? You're not a neophyte
Or some green-inker who can barely spell.
What can I say? I like to be polite.

No, not exactly, Hugo. No, not quite.
I trust this news won't plunge you into hell:
Your rhyme-scheme is some miles from being right.

What's going on? I know you're very bright.
You've won awards. You write supremely well.
What can I say? I like to be polite

And this is true: your books are a delight,
In prose, free verse and letters you excel.
You want my help with getting rhyme-schemes right.

You seem dead keen to master them, despite
Your puzzling inability to tell
Which bit goes where. These lines, if not polite,
Will be of use, I hope. The rhyme-scheme's right.

Two Ann(e)s

for Anne Harvey and Ann Thwaite
(who were at school together)

Anne with an e and Ann without
Were clever girls and good at spelling.
Their teachers couldn't catch them out –
Anne with an e and Ann without.
I hope that you are clear about
Which Ann(e) is which and won't need telling.
Anne with an e and Ann without –
Don't trifle with them. Watch your spelling.

Special Needs

Some pupils here have special needs
Which must be borne in mind.
We monitor them carefully,
In case they fall behind:
The dyslexic, the dyspraxic
And the disinclined.

Old Boys' Day

Row upon row of grey heads
In a chapel built for the young.
I picture them as rows of boys
Who knew, but didn't quite believe,
They would grow old and die.

Once I might have taken them
For sour-faced old buffers.
Now I see they are moved,
That I am not the only person
Who is close to tears.

Yes, there are smiles
Exchanged between friends
When they hear a well-remembered flourish
In the hymn accompaniment
But this is a sombre occasion.

After the service there are drinks,
Warm greetings, an outbreak
Of cheerfulness. It's like the party
After a funeral. And then goodbye –
Goodbye, old chap. Until next year.

Probably

If I'm not sure, I can't say yes.
You need an answer by today.
Probably. Unless. Unless

I've freaked from all the strain and stress,
They've come and carted me away.
If I'm not sure, I can't say yes.

If I'm alive, at this address,
I'll try to do it. I can say
Probably. Unless. Unless

I'm down with flu or in some mess
So dire that I can't work or play.
If I'm not sure, I can't say yes.

I cannot guarantee success.
I'll blow it, forfeiting the pay,
Probably. Unless. Unless

I ask for help in my distress.
Does someone hear me when I pray?
If I'm not sure, I can't say yes.
Probably. Unless. Unless.

Stars

The hotter the star, the bluer it shines.
The smaller the star, the longer it lives.
It shouldn't be hard to remember these lines
(The hotter the star, the bluer it shines).
You can search the night sky for meaningful signs,
Or study it just for the pleasure it gives.
The hotter the star, the bluer it shines.
The smaller the star, the longer it lives.

An Anniversary Poem

tenth anniversary of the ordination of the first women priests in the Church of England in February 1994

Good Christian men and women, let us raise a joyful shout:
The C of E is treating us as equals. Just about.

Sister, fetch the fatted calf, and we'll prepare a feast:
You can't become a bishop but you can become a priest.

The mountains skip like rams, the little hills like sheep.
   And why?
Our problem-solving miracle: a bishop who can fly.

Sing, dance, clap your hands, make merry and be glad:
Some men behave atrociously, but most are not too bad.

Bring out the tambourines, and let the trumpet sound:
These years have not been easy but, praise God, you're still
   around,

Brave, forgiving pioneers. May this be your reward:
To grow in strength and beauty in the service of the Lord.

But should there be a woman Primate while I'm still alive,
Oh, then we'll hear the valleys sing, and see the mountains jive.

'Flying bishops' were appointed for the benefit of male clergy who oppose the ordination of women and are therefore at odds with their diocesan bishop.

Spared

*'That Love is all there is,
Is all we know of Love . . .'*
    – EMILY DICKINSON

It wasn't you, it wasn't me,
Up there, two thousand feet above
A New York street. We're safe and free,
A little while, to live and love,

Imagining what might have been –
The phone-call from the blazing tower,
A last farewell on the machine,
While someone sleeps another hour,

Or worse, perhaps, to say goodbye
And listen to each other's pain,
Send helpless love across the sky,
Knowing we'll never meet again,

Or jump together, hand in hand,
To certain death. Spared all of this
For now, how well I understand
That love is all, is all there is.

Another Valentine

Today we are obliged to be romantic
And think of yet another valentine.
We know the rules and we are both pedantic:
Today's the day we have to be romantic.
Our love is old and sure, not new and frantic.
You know I'm yours and I know you are mine.
And saying that has made me feel romantic,
My dearest love, my darling valentine.

from The Audience

poems commissioned by the Endellion String Quartet

PROLOGUE: THE PERFORMERS

You set off in the morning with a little time to spare.
You should be fine. You should be nice and early getting there.
And everything is hunky-dory till you see a tail
Of traffic that is moving rather slower than a snail.
Ah well, you think, *the chances are I won't be stuck here long.*
This optimistic view turns out to be completely wrong.
And, several hours later, when you limp into the city
Where you need to be, you're fighting off a headache and
    self-pity.
And you know that at the tail end of this long and tiring day
You must sit down in a concert hall, take up your bow
    and play.

The venue sent a map but it's no effing use at all,
So you drive around and drive around until you want to bawl,
Then suddenly you notice that, by chance, you're driving past
Your destination. Turn around, and you've arrived at last.
And, yes, they have a car park but the entrance is behind
The building, round a corner, and it's rather hard to find.
But finally you're parked and you've unloaded all your stuff
And carried it inside. By now you've really had enough.
And you know that at the tail end of this long and tiring day
You must sit down in a concert hall, take up your bow
    and play.

And now there's a rehearsal, interrupted by the need
To get the lighting altered, so that you can see to read,
To fiddle with the music stands, to find some different chairs.
You're trying not to act like rather tender-headed bears.
Then you go off to the green room, which, although it
    doesn't smell,
Does not resemble in the least a luxury hotel.
You change your clothes and comb your hair and hope you
    look all right.
You'd like to have a drink but can't – it's no good getting tight.
For you know that at the tail end of this long and tiring day
You must sit down in the concert hall, take up your bow
    and play.

The auditorium is full, the instruments in tune.
You're feeling slightly nervous. Zero hour is very soon.
You're shepherded towards the wings and there you have to
    pause
Until it's time to enter and acknowledge the applause.
You hope you won't trip over as you walk towards your seat.
You hope you've done your zip up but it's too late to retreat.
The people in the audience are silent as they sit
And wait for something wonderful to happen. This is it.
You sit up straight and you forget your long and tiring day
As you focus on the music and take up your bow and play.

THE COUGHER

There's a tickle in your throat
And you've hardly heard a note
And you're wishing you were in some other place.
In this silent, listening crowd
You're the one who'll cough out loud,
And you know you're facing imminent disgrace.

Yes, right now you're in a pickle.
The unmanageable tickle
Is a torment, and it's threatening your poise.
Can you hold out any longer
As the urge to cough grows stronger?
Any moment you'll emit a mighty noise.

If this bloody piece were shorter,
If you had a glass of water,
It would help. But there is nothing you can do.
Oh, if only you could be
Safe at home with a CD,
In an armchair, free to cough the whole way through.

Do you hear a rallentando?
Does this mean the end's at hand? Oh,
What a mercy. Yes, they're really signing off.
They perform the closing bars
And you thank your lucky stars
And it's over. You have made it. You may cough.

THE TRADITIONALIST

I like a good tune with a regular beat
From the days before music went wrong –
An old-fashioned melody, catchy and sweet.
I like a good tune with a regular beat.
These modern composers, they can't write a song.
They don't get you tapping your feet.
I like a good tune with a regular beat
From the days before music went wrong.

THE RADICAL

I've little patience with this kind of thing –
This trite, post-modern, easy listening.
I hoped for something far more challenging.
This isn't avant-garde enough.
It really isn't hard enough.
It isn't avant-garde enough for me.

The point is not to please the bourgeois ear.
The good composer is a pioneer
Whose music very few will want to hear.
This isn't cutting-edge enough.
It isn't off-the-ledge enough.
It isn't cutting-edge enough for me.

Art should disturb. It's not to make us glad.
It isn't to console us when we're sad.
It's to remind us that the world is bad.
This isn't agonised enough.
You're not antagonised enough.
It isn't agonised enough for me.

Repeat ad lib:
It really isn't hard enough.
It isn't avant-garde enough etc.

THE CRITIC

I hear it once and then I have to write
Six hundred words about it the same night,
Or early in the morning, and submit
A piece displaying polish, wisdom, wit.

It's hard to think of new and different ways
Of being negative or giving praise,
And when you've penned a decade of reviews
You're sick of all the adjectives you use.

Exquisite, brilliant, superb, first-rate.
Impressive, masterly, outstanding, great,
Inept, monotonous, indifferent, bad.
Atrocious, terrible, sub-standard, mad,

And so on. I work hard to make it just,
To be the kind of critic you can trust.
I do my very best. I send it in.
One day's exposure. Then it's in the bin.

FIRST DATE

She

I said I liked classical music.
It wasn't exactly a lie.
I hoped he would get the impression
That my brow was acceptably high.

I said I liked classical music.
I mentioned Vivaldi and Bach.
And he asked me along to this concert.
Here we are, sitting in the half-dark.

I was thrilled to be asked to the concert.
I couldn't decide what to wear.
I hope I look tastefully sexy.
I've done what I can with my hair.

Yes, I'm thrilled to be here at this concert.
I couldn't care less what they play
But I'm trying my hardest to listen
So I'll have something clever to say.

When I glance at his face it's a picture
Of rapt concentration. I see
He is totally into this music
And quite undistracted by me.

FIRST DATE

He

She said she liked classical music.
I implied I was keen on it too.
Though I don't often go to a concert,
It wasn't entirely untrue.

I looked for a suitable concert
And here we are, on our first date.
The traffic was dreadful this evening
And I arrived ten minutes late.

So we haven't had much time for talking
And I'm a bit nervous. I see
She is totally lost in the music
And quite undistracted by me.

In that dress she is very attractive –
The neckline can't fail to intrigue.
I mustn't appear too besotted.
Perhaps she is out of my league.

Where are we? I glance at the programme
But I've put my glasses away.
I'd better start paying attention
Or else I'll have nothing to say.

THE WIDOW

I like this piece. I think you'd like it too.
We didn't very often disagree
Back in the days when I sat here with you
And knew that you were coming home with me.
This is the future. It arrived so fast.
When we were young it seemed so far away.
Our years together vanished like a day
At nightfall, sealed forever in the past.
I can't give up on music, just discard
The interest we shared because you died.
And so I come to concerts. But it's hard.
Tonight I'm doing well. I haven't cried.
My head aches. There's a tightness in my throat.
And you will never hear another note.

A Rehearsal

for Roxanna Panufnik and the Endellion String Quartet

How shall we play this? We have all got votes,
The six of us rehearsing here today.
Hang on a minute. Can I check my notes?
You want a B flat here? You're sure? OK.

Six of us rehearsing here today,
Composer, poet and a string quartet
(You want a creaky sound? Like this? OK),
And do we all have points to make? You bet.

Composer, poet and a string quartet –
The poet has a *role* as the narrator –
And do we all have points to make? You bet.
Too fast. Too loud. You need to come in later.

The poet has a *role* as the narrator.
Her lips are moving as she tries to count.
Bar 92. You need to come in later.
We have some little problems to surmount.

Her lips are moving as she tries to count.
The first performance is a week away.
We have some little problems to surmount.
It's going to be fine. That's what we say.

The first performance is a week away.
Now shall we play it through? We've all got votes.
It's going to be fine. That's what we say.
Hang on a minute. Can I check my notes?

from An ABC of the BBC

poems commissioned by BBC Radio 4

THE ARCHERS AND ADULTERY

I like *The Archers* only when it's got
Adulterous behaviour in the plot.
Just when it was becoming one long yawn
They gave us – yippee! – Brian and Siobhan.
I was delighted. I did not care tuppence
When smug, kept Jennifer got her comeuppance.

Then there was Ruth's flirtation. Would she do it
With Sam? Of course she wouldn't and I knew it.
I said it all along. I had no doubt.
She got to the hotel and bottled out.
So now she'll be a good, upstanding wife
('Oh, no!') six episodes a week for life.

She'll be like all the other Archers, who
Like nothing better than a family do,
With everyone together. Young and old
Content to be within the family fold,
With no one wishing that they could avoid it,
And everybody saying they enjoyed it.

Yes, in *The Archers* family values reign.
The straying spouses all come back again.
Sam disappeared and poor Siobhan is dead
And we get problems with the cows instead.
I listen sometimes, doing random checks,
So I'll know when there's more illicit sex.

DIGITAL AND INTERACTIVE

for Julian May

The producer wants me to write about digital and interactive.
I have tried but I do not find these subjects attractive.
There is a gap and this attempt to bridge it'll
Be all there is on interactive or on digital.

FOOTBALL

A most delightful programme
Goes out on Saturday
When football fans ring Radio 5,
All keen to have their say.

Caller after caller
Whose team is doing badly
Will tell us what the problem is,
More angrily than sadly.

There are two explanations
For failure, as a rule:
The referee's a villain or
The manager's a fool.

The Radio 5 presenter
Is rational and calm,
Defending refs against the men
Who want to do them harm,

Who want them to be punished
For their defective vision –
Dismissed, disgraced and disembowelled
For every bad decision.

The righteous rage! The passion!
I'm not a football fan
But this is first-rate comedy.
I listen when I can.

THE MIDDLE CLASSES

When BBC top brasses
Play games with Radio 4,
The angry middle classes
Rise up and say 'No more!'

'Don't meddle with our programmes,
Don't change a thing because
We are your faithful listeners.
We liked it as it was.'

The weeks go by. We settle,
Recover from the shock
Of learning that *The Archers*
Is now at two o'clock,

And we adjust our habits.
Astonishingly soon,
We don't recall that *Woman's Hour*
Was in the afternoon.

But if some new controller
Starts changing things again
You can be sure we'll have our say,
Protest with voice and pen.

And so the decade passes,
As decades did of yore.
Long live the middle classes
And long live Radio 4.

QUIZZES

I'm always glad when there's a quiz
To make my little brain cells fizz.
I get to show off all my wealth
Of general knowledge to myself.

But, any time I'm asked to go
And take part on the radio,
I straight away decline the chance
To show off all my ignorance.

UNBEARABLE
or THINGS THAT MAKE ME SWITCH THE RADIO OFF

Talk of scary medical conditions,
Clichés from the mouths of politicians,

Interviewers whose self-righteous tone
Suggests they have the right to cast a stone,

Too much aggression early in the day
(Just press a switch and it will go away),

Reporters whose command of English grammar
Deserves a beta minus or a gamma,

Comedians making unkind jokes about
A person's looks (no thank you; count me out),

Actors being actorish, and, worse,
The voice of Dylan Thomas reading verse.

X-RATED

for Horatio Clare

If someone wants to use a naughty word
The rule is that it has to be referred
To someone higher up, who must decide
If saying the said word is justified.

Some listeners, of course, will have a fit
If anyone's permitted to say it
And lots of people will be horror-struck
To hear the BBC broadcasting muck.

So there's a person in an office who
Considers all those words for me and you.
The same old words come back and back again –
She probably employs them now and then.

CLOSEDOWN

for Alice Arnold

An almost empty building:
Someone, all alone,
Reads the shipping forecast
To a microphone.

Listeners in bedrooms,
Listeners at sea,
Thousands of them, hear her
Speak invisibly,

Hear her through the darkness,
Hear her say goodnight,
Picture her alone there,
Switching off the light.

Is it really like that?
I asked if I could go
And be with the announcer
In the studio.

And, yes, it's really like that.
Someone, all alone,
Reads the shipping forecast
To a microphone,

Speaks into the darkness,
Says a last goodnight,
Plays the national anthem,
Switches off the light.

UNCOLLECTED POEMS

— 2001–2009 —

Forty-seven Words

for LM

Thanks for putting up with me.
The best years were with you –
So kind, and such good company.
Thanks for putting up with me.
By loving me, you helped me be
A loving person too.
Thanks for putting up with me.
Best thing of all was you.

Commissioned for *You have breath for no more than 99 words. What would they be?* (Darton, Longman and Todd, 2011).

After Heine

ICH GLAUB NICHT AN DEN HIMMEL

I don't believe in Heaven,
Whatever the preachers say.
I've only your beloved eyes
To light me on my way.

They talk of God the Father –
I don't believe he's there.
You love me and the joyful news
Is with me everywhere.

I don't believe in Satan
Or in the fires of Hell.
Your cold eyes, your indifference –
They'll do just as well.

ICH HAB IM TRAUM GEWEINET

I dreamed that I was weeping,
I dreamed that you had died.
I woke. A teardrop told me
That I had really cried.

I dreamed that I was weeping –
You'd gone away from me.
I woke and went on crying
A long time, bitterly.

I dreamed that I was weeping.
I dreamed you hadn't gone.
I woke. The tears were streaming
And they go on and on.

HERZ, MEIN HERZ, SEI NICHT BEKLOMMEN

Heart, my heart, do not be prey
To misery. Accept your fate.
Spring will give back, if you wait,
What the winter took away.

And so much is with you still.
The lovely world is yours to treasure
And, whatever gives you pleasure,
You may love it, love it all.

Sporty People

I took her for my kind of person
And it was something of a shock
When my new friend revealed
That, once upon a time,
She was a junior county tennis champion.

How could that happen?
How could I accidentally
Make friends with a tennis champion?
How could a tennis champion
Make friends with me?

She wasn't stupid. She read books.
She had never been mean to me
For being bad at games.
I decided to forgive
Her unfortunate past.

Sporty people can be OK –
Of course they can.
Later on, I met poets
Who played football. It's still hard
To get my head round that.

Travel Sonnet

Don't want to go away. I never do
The day, the week before I have to leave.
Now, I'd give anything to stay with you
But it's too late. Today I pack. And grieve –
As if it were our very last day ever,
As if I knew that one of us would die
This week and it were certain we would never
Be reunited. Pack and pack and cry.
How foolish to accept the invitation
To fly so far away all on my own,
Agreeing to this painful separation,
To heading friendless into the unknown.
It may be wonderful. It often is.
But first I have to drag myself through this.

from CHRISTMAS POEMS

— 2017 —

Christmas Triolet

for Gavin Ewart

It's Christmas, season of wild bells
And merry carols. On the floor
Are gifts in pretty paper shells.
It's Christmas, season of wild Belle's
Big party. George's stomach swells
With ale; his wife's had even more.
It's Christmas, season of wild belles,
And merry Carol's on the floor.

Motorway Music

At last, in spite of everything,
The moment does arrive.
This year it was on Christmas Eve,
Teatime, M25,

When I switched on the radio
And heard 'Nowell, Nowell',
And had to join in, singing for
The King of Israel,

Along with half the choirs on earth
And all the choirs of Heaven,
As I drove through the pouring rain,
Approaching Junction 7.

And then my passenger woke up
And came in with his bass.
I wanted to see happiness
Like ours on every face

In every car. The traffic slowed.
The queue went on and on.
The sound of trumpets introduced
Another Christmas song.

Who cares about a traffic jam
While herald angels sing?
Each year the moment does arrive,
In spite of everything.

Bethlehem

There stands a church in Bethlehem today,
Built where the baby in the manger lay,
Where Mary touched and kissed his little face:
A place of pilgrimage, a holy place.

O holy Jesus, Everlasting Light,
Let there be peace in Bethlehem tonight.

And once, in better times, I travelled there,
Watched children run around in Manger Square,
Then went into the church's crypt and stood
Before the birthplace of the Son of God.

O holy Jesus, Everlasting Light,
Let there be peace in Bethlehem tonight.

Now, in the little town where Christ was born,
Young men and children die, and mothers mourn.
Wise men have not brought peace to Manger Square.
O hear us as we offer up this prayer:

O holy Jesus, Everlasting Light,
Let there be peace in Bethlehem tonight.

ANECDOTAL EVIDENCE
— 2018 —

Evidence

'A great deal of anecdotal evidence suggests that we respond positively to birdsong.'
　　– scientific researcher, *Daily Telegraph*, 8 February 2012

　　　　Centuries of English verse
　　　　Suggest the selfsame thing:
　　　　A negative response is rare
　　　　When birds are heard to sing.

　　　　What's the use of poetry?
　　　　You ask. Well, here's a start:
　　　　It's anecdotal evidence
　　　　About the human heart.

The Damage to the Piano

You can barely see
the damage to the piano
where the new bookcase knocked it,
but all hell would break loose
if my mother were here.

I sit for several minutes,
pondering the silence
where I am cast adrift
with all this furniture
and no one to tell me off.

Baggage

Two smart porters carry luggage on
The label from the Nacional, Madrid.
The one from the hotel in Carcassonne
Features the fortress. That's stuck on the lid.
Some are partly missing. This one here
Says Vichy, and another Lac de Co . . .
Some scraps remain mysterious as to where
My father travelled all those years ago.
His sturdy leather suitcase, left too long
In our damp garage, still looks glamorous
To me. It calls to mind the handsome, young
And happy man I'd like to think he was.
The child of his old age, I close my eyes
And join him under sunny foreign skies.

Orb

An illuminated orb
against a black background –
the colour of flesh, with faint
red lines that could be rivers.

Not a planet in the night sky:
my eyeball
on the optician's screen.

It's beautiful. Just one small feature
of a mysterious universe
I'll never explore, packed neatly
in this soft container.

We know so little of ourselves,
and of each other – the working parts
we carry everywhere,

the darkness we scan
like astronomers, seeking
the half-forgotten stories of our lives.

1952

Sometimes, instead of a farthing,
shops give you safety pins.
Can that be right? I'm sure
it's what the teacher said.

I know it was 1952
because the same teacher, a nun,
announced one morning
that the King had died.

We were encouraged to go
to the chapel, to pray for his soul.
A Catholic friend showed me
what you do with the holy water.

It was lovely in there –
white, gold, pastels –
as pretty as the scenery
for the last act of a pantomime.

It may have been the same day
that I upset my mother
by asking for a rosary.
Soon after that,

as we sat down in a theatre,
where I couldn't make a fuss,
she told me it had been decided:
boarding school, next term.

Bags

After all these years
I've begun using it again –
the laundry bag embroidered
by Nanna: W. M. COPE LINEN
in large, neat red letters.

There's another bag somewhere,
a smaller one, with
W. M. COPE SHOES
embroidered in purple.
I've been trying to find it

to carry my shoes in
while snow is on the ground.
I have other fabric bags –
dozens of cotton ones
from libraries and festivals –

but I want the one Nanna made,
the one that hung in a cold
cloakroom until it was time
to pull on wellingtons
and trudge up the path to lessons.

I see that little girl
on an icy morning, with her shoe bag,
and I think of the grandmother
who couldn't prevent her
from being sent away

but spent hours making
things she could take with her
when she went to a place
where she didn't know anyone
and nobody knew her name.

Upheavals

When I was home in the holidays
I dreaded going back to school.
On the last day my mother and I
usually doubled our unhappiness
by having a row about the packing.

Once I had settled down at school,
I was fine. I didn't long for home
or for my parents until,
on a couple of Saturdays every term,
they came to take me out.

Sometimes we went to Lympne Airport
and watched cars being loaded
on to planes. The nose opened
and they went in from the front,
like something being swallowed by a whale –

a whale that could lift itself
and its heavy load into the air
for the short journey to France.
It was interesting enough to lift
my spirits a little. And there was tea.

But I remember those Saturdays
as heavy with the knowledge
that they would soon be over,
with the thought of parting
and homesickness and tears.

As I launched myself once more
into school life with friends
and teachers, the burden grew lighter.
I was all right. I wished
my parents would leave me alone.

Absent Friends

*'The ones we remember are those linked
with things we do all the time'*
— KATHARINE WHITEHORN

ROZ

My schoolfriend Roz, who died twenty years ago,
pulled her cardigan down at the back
every time she stood up and crossed a room.

Whenever I glance in a mirror
and see that my cardigan has ridden up
I remember Roz.

She was my rival in English.
The teachers were so impressed
by her passion for Tolkien
that I didn't read *The Lord of the Rings*
until I was fifty-five.

JULIA

I

Julia, dear Julia,
taught me, one afternoon
in a shop in Chislehurst,
how to choose a card.
'That one is vulgar.
This one is too sweet.'

She's dead now
but her taste lives on.
I never buy a birthday or
a Christmas card
without asking myself
if she would approve.

2

She rang me in the holidays
and told me she was doing
a chapter of Caesar every day.
I followed her example
and passed the exam.

The last time I saw her
she was dying, bravely,
of motor neurone disease.
She couldn't speak. She wrote notes
that made us laugh.

That's an example
I may need to follow one day –
harder than translating Caesar,
but, if I think of Julia,
perhaps I'll pass the test.

Reunion

Fifty years have passed since we first met,
And forty-seven since we said goodbye,
Embarking on our adult lives – and yet
You are the same, it seems to me. Am I?
Five decades of life, of ups and downs,
Of love and marriage, work and motherhood,
And here we are, back in the world of gowns
And college food and essays – and it's good,
It's very good, my lovely, clever friends,
To travel to the past and find you here,
To share just one more evening meal that ends
In someone's room – before we disappear
Into a future, where I'm sad to know
It's over. It was over long ago.

An Afternoon

The two of them are sitting on the bed
In my small student room. My second year.
My parents are both feeling very sad
After a funeral not far from here:
My mother's closest girlhood friend, who died
Of cancer in her forties. They agree
They can't face driving home just yet, decide
To come and spend an hour or two with me.
And I, for once, am genuinely pleased
To see them. I'm depressed. I haven't said.
I hope the hugs and smiles I gave them eased
Their grief. Years later, when they're dead,
I will remember and be moved to say
I never loved them more than on that day.

1972

It was the year
of the hippy librarians from Islington.
My flatmate met hers first
and I got off with his friend.

They had beards. They smoked dope.
They were very alternative.
Mine gave me a copy
of *Vedanta for the Western World*.

I wore long Indian dresses
and tried to like the smell of joss sticks.
In August we sat in bed
and watched the Olympics, stoned.

Late that year I went into analysis.
Freud didn't get along
with the hippy boyfriend.
We drifted apart.

It was fun, some of the time,
while it lasted. You could say that,
I suppose, about most years,
about most lives.

Memorial

When I got home from Aunty Bob's funeral
I began to write a poem about her
but the man I was in love with phoned
and asked me out. I abandoned the poem
and never went back to it.

Miss Tucker. That was what they called her
in the shop. She was in charge
of haberdashery. Customers noticed
that she got on well with Mr Cartwright
of men's outfitting. A match, perhaps?

They had been married to each other
for years. He was Uncle Maurice,
a veteran of World War I, who never
mentioned it except to tell us, with a laugh,
that they all said 'Wipers' instead of 'Ypres'.

They laughed a lot, those two.
He recited comic monologues
as a party turn – 'Yon Lion's et Albert' –
and taught my sister to play pontoon.
Mummy wasn't happy about that.

They loved me and were always kind.
I loved them too. So, here's a small
memorial, three decades overdue.
The man who phoned? That didn't work out.
I wrote a dozen poems about him.

A Vow

I cannot promise never to be angry;
I cannot promise always to be kind.
You know what you are taking on, my darling –
It's only at the start that love is blind.

And yet I'm still the one you want to be with
And you're the one for me – of that I'm sure.
You are my closest friend, my favourite person,
The lover and the home I've waited for.

I cannot promise that I will deserve you
From this day on. I hope to pass that test.
I love you and I want to make you happy.
I promise I will do my very best.

To My Husband

If we were never going to die, I might
Not hug you quite as often or as tight,
Or say goodbye to you as carefully
If I were certain you'd come back to me.
Perhaps I wouldn't value every day,
Every act of kindness, every laugh
As much, if I knew you and I could stay
For ever as each other's other half.
We may not have too many years before
One disappears to the eternal yonder
And I can't hug or touch you any more.
Yes, of course that knowledge makes us fonder.
Would I want to change things, if I could,
And make us both immortal? Love, I would.

Calculations

I have been a non-smoker, now, for longer
                          than I was a smoker.

I have been a published poet almost as long
                          as I wasn't.

For more than half my adult years, I have earned a living
                          without having a job.

I have been fatherless for nearly two-thirds of my life.

In the run-up to our wedding I reflect that I will not be
                a married woman for half as long as I was single.

But, if we are both alive when I am 96, I will have had
                as many years with you as without you –

nearly a third of my life so far.

With luck, the fraction will grow, like evening sunlight
                          spreading across a field,

so the view at the end of the day is brighter and more
                                  beautiful

than I could have foreseen in the long, dark hours of
                                the morning.

One Day

One day, my love, the good times will be over,
Never to return. And it could come
Quite suddenly – the news that either one
Of us is ill, unlikely to recover.
How will we deal with that – day after day
Of grief and sickness? Will we both be brave
And kind in everything we do and say
And, failing that, be able to forgive?
We'll have to do our best to stay afloat,
Despite our anger, tiredness and fear,
Trusting in our love, a sturdy boat
That's served us pretty well, year after year.
We'll hope it can survive the stormy weather
And bring us safely into port, together.

The Tree

We had to leave our home. We travelled here
With all our worldly goods – box after box
Of crockery and books, our furniture,
Our pictures, mirrors, lamps and rugs and clocks.
In its pot our precious Christmas tree,
A straggly adolescent, four years old,
Survived the journey, waited patiently
Till it was time to come in from the cold.
Now it's lit up in all its annual glory,
Hung with treasures taken out of store.
Every little trinket tells a story,
A memoir of the life we had before.
We got through the disruption and the pain.
The tree is telling us we're home again.

Here We Are

Here we are
in our small, chosen city,
happy to watch the ducks,
the narrowboats, the changing trees.

On the other side of the river
long goods trains trundle past.
Maersk, China Shipping,
China Shipping, Maersk.

Big world out there.
Ports, oceans, shopping districts.

We could be anywhere
but this is where we find ourselves,
happy to sit beside the river
and watch the trains go by.

Ely

for Mac Dowdy, historian

We thought our little city got its name
From eels. They have been caught and traded here
For centuries. The Isle of Eels became
The Isle of Ely. We liked that idea.
But there's a problem, since the word for eel,
Back when the early settlement was founded,
Was *anguilla* or *schlippen-fisch* or *aal*,
And no one spoke of eels till 1300.
A newer theory, out of academe:
In ancient times this place was venerated
As holy, as a paradise. Its name,
As years went by, became abbreviated.
We like this even better: our new home
Is in a city called Elysium.

March 2013

The winter's going on and on.
The daffodils refuse to flower.
Like us, they're waiting for the sun.

They hug themselves inside the green
Through every icy gale and shower –
Through winter, going on and on.

St David's day has come and gone
And still they're waiting for the hour
When they can open in the sun.

One afternoon last week it shone
And briefly cheered us up before
It vanished. Winter's going on.

The sick and dying wonder when
The spring will come. Will they be here
When it arrives, with flowers and sun?

They hoped to see another one.
The skies aren't answering their prayer.
The winter's going on and on.
Like us, they're waiting for the sun.

Haiku: Willows

Willows white with frost:
like fireworks that whooshed, sparkled
and froze in the air.

Naga-Uta

Clearest of clear days:
frozen leaves under my feet,
frost on bare branches,
blue sky, smoke from the funnel
of a narrowboat,
and on the quiet river
great slicks of pale gold sunlight.

Naga-uta is a Japanese form

By the River

The day is so still
you can almost hear the heat.
You can almost hear
that royal blue dragonfly
landing on the old white boat.

Shakespeare at School

Forty boys on benches with their quills
Six days a week through almost all the year,
Long hours of Latin with relentless drills
And repetition, all enforced by fear.
I picture Shakespeare sitting near the back,
Indulging in a risky bit of fun
By exercising his prodigious knack
Of thinking up an idiotic pun,
And whispering his gem to other boys,
Some of whom could not suppress their mirth –
Behaviour that unfailingly annoys
Any teacher anywhere on earth.
The fun was over when the master spoke:
Will Shakespeare, come up here and share the joke.

The Marriage

Married at eighteen to a pregnant bride
Eight years your senior, did you think that you
Had spoiled your life before you'd even tried
To make your way and show what you could do?
Perhaps you loved each other and were glad
To tie the knot. Perhaps, each time you left
Your Anne, your little daughters and the lad
To set out on the road, you were bereft.
Perhaps you were relieved to get away.
Perhaps she was relieved to see you go.
Did you miss each other every day
And long for the return? We cannot know
The cost to you, your family, your wife.
We cannot wish you'd lived a different life.

On Sonnet 18

'So long as men can breathe and eyes can see' –
You don't assume we'll be around for ever.
You couldn't know that 'this gives life to thee'
Only until the sun goes supernova.
That knowledge doesn't prove your words untrue.
Neither time nor the advance of science
Has taken anything away from you,
Or faced down your magnificent defiance.
That couplet. Were you smiling as you wrote it?
Did you utter a triumphant 'Yes'?
Walking round the garden, did you quote it,
Sotto voce, savouring your success?
And did you always know, or sometimes doubt,
That passing centuries would bear you out?

The Worst Row

The worst row we two ever had concerned
The sonnets – Shakespeare's. I expressed the view
I'd held for years: that no one could have turned
Those lines unless he was in love. 'Not true.
You'll find that all the academics say
You're wrong.' That pompous tone – the one that you
Use when you'll brook no argument. 'And they
Know better than mere poets?' 'Yes, they do.'
It happened in the car. I nearly stopped
And asked you to get out. Now I concede
That both of us were partly right. We dropped
The sulks before too long. But we're agreed
It was our worst dispute. The one we had
About a steak? That wasn't quite as bad.

My Father's Shakespeare

My father must have bought it secondhand,
Inscribed 'To R. S. Elwyn' – who was he?
Published 1890, leather-bound,
In 1961 passed on to me.
November 6th. How old was I? Sixteen.
Doing A level in English Lit.,
In love with Keats and getting very keen
On William Shakespeare. I was thrilled with it,
This gift, glad then, as now, to think
I had been chosen as the keeper of
My father's Shakespeare, where, in dark blue ink,
He wrote, 'To Wendy Mary Cope. With love.'
Love on a page, surviving death and time.
He didn't even have to make it rhyme.

At New Place

Not the one he planted but its 'scion',
According to the plaque, which I peruse
Close up, absorbed. I fail to keep an eye on
My feet till mulberry juice has ruined my shoes.
Pale grey lace-ups. Dark red fallen fruit.
And it's all Shakespeare's fault. If only he
Had chosen something different for this spot –
An oak, a sycamore, an apple tree.
I sit down on a nearby bench and think
Of Shakespeare with a sapling and a spade
And how this incident creates a link
Between us in the garden that he made.
I feel him smiling at me as he says
'Oh yes. The Muse works in mysterious ways.'

Young Love

School outing, 1960: *Romeo*
And Juliet. First time I'd seen a play
By Shakespeare on the stage. We had to go
By bus to the Old Vic. A matinee.
Don't know what I expected, probably
To find it rather boring. It was not.
Enchanted, I went back four times to see
The play again. I was in love. With what?
The characters (Mercutio!)? The actors –
Judi Dench and several dishy males?
The language? Maybe all of them were factors
Compelling me to boost the ticket sales
For Shakespeare plays as often as I could.
That teenage crush: I think it did me good.

If It Be Now

If it be now, 'tis not to come:
Hamlet, just before the fight
That sent him to eternal night.

It's always there: a quiet drum
Sounding when I have a fright:
If it be now, 'tis not to come.

Choking, breathless, falling – numb
With mortal fear, I hear it right
On cue and silently recite,
If it be now, 'tis not to come.

In Memory of Max Adrian 1903–1973

It's sad to think the actor never knew
About the teenage girl who saw him play
In *As You Like It* long ago and who
Can still recall his face and voice today:
His Jaques dignified, aloof and dry –
No bellowing, no sawing of the air,
Nothing that could offend the author's eye
Or ear, if you imagined he was there.
More than fifty years have passed since then
But when I read the text it's him I see,
And when I watch it on the stage again
Jaques doesn't stand a chance with me.
Max nailed the part and no one else will do.
And that, it's possible to hope, he knew.

On Sonnet 22

My glass can't quite persuade me I am old –
In that respect my ageing eyes are kind –
But when I see a photograph, I'm told
The dismal truth: I've left my youth behind.
And when I try to get up from a chair
My knees remind me they are past their best.
The burden they have carried everywhere
Is heavier now. No wonder they protest.
Arthritic fingers, problematic neck,
Sometimes causing mild to moderate pain,
Could well persuade me I'm an ancient wreck
But here's what helps me to feel young again:
My love, who fell for me so long ago,
Still loves me just as much, and tells me so.

A Wreath for George Herbert

Dear George, although I do not share your faith,
A faith expressed in poems I revere,
Revere and love, I offer you this wreath,
A wreath of words, like yours, although I fear,
I fear it won't be worthy of the man,
The awe-inspiring man who loved to play,
To play with words, to make them rhyme and scan,
Scan and rhyme and at the same time say,
Say something true: the truth about your fear,
Your fear, your anger and your love. A wreath,
A humble wreath for someone I revere,
Revere and love, though I can't share your faith.

A Poem about Jesus

When I find myself feeling sorry for the wrong people –
disgraced politicians, vilified bankers,
the victims of paedophile witch-hunts –
I remember that Jesus was the friend of sinners
and he would have felt sorry for them too.

I love him for that. And I love him
for being on the side of the wusses,
telling us the meek will inherit the earth.

I don't know if he was the son of God.
I don't know if he rose from the grave.
If he is a fiction,
the genius who created him
deserves all the love and the praise we can give.

Little Donkey

The children's favourite. We had
to sing it in the Christmas concert
every year, plodding along
with me at the piano, and a child
going clip-clop with coconut shells
or woodblock: a coveted job.

It wasn't my favourite.
After I left teaching
I forgot about it
for more than ten years

until one day, near Christmas,
in a busy high street
a Salvation Army band
began to play it. I stood still

with tears in my eyes.
'Little Donkey'. All those children
who loved it so much.
All those hands in the air
begging to be chosen
to make the sound of his hooves.

Lantern Carol

At the winter solstice,
Midnight of the year,
A lantern in a stable
Shows us He is here.

Shining through the ages,
Lighting up the place
Where we see the baby,
His little hands, his face,

A lantern in a stable
Centuries ago
Conquers time and darkness
With its gentle glow,

Calls us with the shepherds
And the eastern kings,
Offers us the Christ child
And the love He brings.

In the golden lamplight,
See him there asleep.
Ours if we will have Him.
Ours to love and keep.

Christmas Cards

Cards to the very old
go out like doves
who will bring back news
of one kind or another.

It may be a sign of life –
a few sentences
in a shaky hand,
I hope that you are well.

It may be a letter
from a friend or relative
who found my address on the back:
I am very sorry to tell you . . .

This year two cards,
both to widowers,
came winging back with labels:
Addressee gone away.

I open my Christmas list,
find their names
and type *d.2016.*
I could remove them

but that would leave
no trace of them
and I am not quite ready
for them to disappear.

In Memory of Dennis O'Driscoll

After I heard that you had died
I went and found your Christmas card –
People round a tree.
Inside, a message written days
Before, and all in upper case,
Of course, for L. and me.

You mention 'Our reunion
In Dublin'. That took place in June –
A reading on a date
When all of Ireland had to see
A football match. Our poetry
Could not compete with that.

It didn't matter much to me.
I'd flown across the Irish Sea
Because you asked me to,
Though not imagining, dear friend,
That you had nearly reached the end
Until I looked at you –

So very thin, so very pale.
How could you not be gravely ill?
You said you were OK –
Some minor problem, sorted now.
Whatever else you feared or knew
You were not going to say.

No more envelopes from you,
Bold capitals announcing who
Had written us a letter.
Those letters were so generous
With warmth, intelligence and praise,
They made us both feel better.

I hope you knew how much it meant –
Your interest, your encouragement.
I hope I made it clear
That you were high up on my list
Of favourite people. You'll be missed
As long as I am here.

In Memory of a Psychoanalyst

Arthur S. Couch 1924–2015

1   THE KLEINIANS

Your funeral. And on the day
The Kleinians were crying.
Your vilified opponents. They
Turned up for you on that sad day
And wept. I wonder what you'd say –
Some quip about the perks of dying?
I wish you knew that on the day
The Kleinians were crying.

2   DREAMS

I had a dream about Nanna.
I was walking in her funeral procession
and she was walking beside me,
alive and well.

You talked about ambivalence:
I wanted her back
but I was tired
of worrying about her.

I had a dream about you,
a dream I won't be telling you,
now you're gone, now
I can only tell the page.

You came to see us, you
and a friend, a woman analyst.
We sat and talked. It was
a pleasant occasion.

When you left, you walked
a little way, then turned to wave.
That image of you, well and happy,
has brought you back

the way you were before
your wife died, before
the years of loneliness,
before you were ill.

It seems (as you would say)
it seems I have a wish
to see you restored to health
and with a companion,

a wish for you to visit me
and meet my husband,
to stay a little while
and then go cheerfully away.

I miss you sometimes
but I'm not felled by grief.
It seems that's how it should be.
It seems you did a good job.

A Little Tribute to John Cage

'Wherever we are, what we hear is mostly noise. When we ignore it, it disturbs us. When we listen to it, we find it fascinating.'
– JOHN CAGE

My computer humming
while triangles dance on the screen.

A blackbird singing,
perched on the garden gate.

The soft scratch of my pencil
as I write these words.

A trio for computer,
blackbird and pencil.

One continuous sound, one random,
one controlled by me.

The pencil's part is almost over.
When it stops

A Statue

Here is a statue of a man who died
Nearly thirty years ago. He stands
On one leg, in a dancing pose, beside
The sea, near children playing on the sands.
People with cameras form a little queue.
In turn the men adopt the dancing pose.
I'm touched to see what all the women do:
They hug the statue's arm and nestle close.
Is there another statue anywhere
That people treat like this? Can't think of one.
The man wears specs, has lost most of his hair,
Inspires affection that goes on and on.
The town? The man? Both answers are the same:
Morecambe. Eric Morecambe is the name.

Cento

for Fleur Adcock

Art's whatever you choose to frame.
It looks easy enough. Let's try it.

I got a Gold Star for the Pilgrim Fathers
but I don't suppose that counts, does it?

In the dream I was kissing John Prescott.
No one ever notices his ears.

All the worse things come stalking in
and I am still a day off 70.

Somehow we manage to like our friends,
but now that I am in love with a place

one day is enough to remember.
It makes me laugh. In fact, it makes me sing.

A cento is a verse composition made up of lines from existing poems. These are all by Fleur Adcock.

Where's a Pied Piper When You Need One?

headline in the Daily Telegraph, *25 May 2012*

In 'The Pied Piper of Hamelin' by Robert Browning
Thousands of rats are led to the river and to death
   by drowning.
A good story but not a true one: no one sensible believes
   a word of it.
Nonetheless, tourists flock to Hamelin because they have
   heard of it.
Tourists spend money and make a place richer,
But, sad to recount, that is not the whole picher.
Visitors leave litter, some of it edible, and that's
Why Hamelin has a problem, and the problem is RATS.
When they've finished their dinner they go back underground
And gnaw through any cables that are lying around.
The traffic lights stop working and so does the fountain.
Council workmen have repaired them so many times they
   have stopped countin',
Which brings me at last to the burden of my song:
Next time someone quotes Auden saying 'Poetry makes
   nothing happen', you can tell them he was wrong.

On a Photograph of the Archbishop of Canterbury

You see an archbishop out jogging in shorts.
You know it's unfair to have negative thoughts.

There's no reason at all why he shouldn't keep fit.
It's commendable. You can't help sneering a bit

And thinking of Becket and Cranmer and Laud
And numerous others, who may have been flawed,

But of whom, I believe it is safe to say, none
Ever took off his trousers and went for a run.

Of course, things are tough for archbishops today –
Nasty photographers snapping away.

It's nasty of me to write this. I confess it.
I don't think I'm sorry enough to suppress it.

Men Talking

Anecdotes and jokes,
On and on and on.
If you're with several blokes,
It's anecdotes and jokes.

If you were to die
Of boredom, there and then,
They'd notice, by and by,
If you were to die.

But it could take a while.
They're having so much fun.
You neither speak nor smile.
It could take a while.

At 70

after W. S. Gilbert

Of fitness and vitality I am not the epitome.
I sometimes think there's something wrong with nearly every
    bit o' me.
My teeth are wearing out. I cannot give them a sabbatical,
And finding shoes that will not hurt my feet is problematical.
My hearing isn't what it was. I fear that's undeniable.
My memory? It may be just a fraction less reliable.
I cannot read a word unless my glasses are available.
The view that I am somewhat overweight is unassailable.

That's been a lifelong struggle. I'm not ready to surrender yet.
I'm very careful what I eat. I dream that I'll be slender yet.
I might stay healthy longer if I were a vegetarian,
But I'm not doing badly for a septuagenarian.

My blood tests came back fine when they were sent off
    for analysis.
I'm lucky not to be on chemo or to need dialysis.
My hips and knees are bearing up. They do not want
    replacing yet
And cardiac anxieties are something I'm not facing yet.
It might be better for my health if I were less dogmatical
And didn't freak out when a news report is ungrammatical
Or when a word is mispronounced. If someone says
    'mischievious',
I want to shake them and explain it doesn't rhyme with
    devious.

Please don't call me sprightly, as I may react aggressively
And use my sprightly tongue to speak a little too expressively.
Perhaps I am intolerant, a tad authoritarian,
But I'm not doing badly for a septuagenarian.

I do some boring exercises to improve mobility.
I don't know if there's anything that helps postpone senility.
I do a crossword every day. I play with forms poetical –
With one as tough as this I sometimes get a bit frenetical.
I borrowed it from Gilbert's lines about the 'Major-Gineral',
Where even Gilbert had to cheat to make it rhyme with mineral,
Since nothing rhymes with General. The problem was intractable
But no one minds because his song's so singable and actable.

Gilbert was a genius who always got the metre right.
It is my modest hope that I have counted up these feet aright.
Where prosody's concerned, I've never been a libertarian
And I'm not changing now that I'm a septuagenarian.

Health Advice

'People who read books enjoy a significant "survival advantage" over those who do not.'
— report in *The Times*, 5 August 2016, on a survey published in *Social Science and Medicine*

> If you want to stay alive,
> Sit and read a book.
> It will help you to survive.
> If you want to stay alive,
> Eat broccoli and you may thrive
> But here's the good news – look:
> If you want to stay alive,
> Sit and read a book.

New Year

The year has died. Another year is born
And people party, set the sky ablaze.
Puzzled by their happiness, I mourn
The passing of so many precious days.
Enjoyed or squandered, they won't come again.
Out there the world is celebrating. Why?
The solemn midnight tolling of Big Ben
Tells us we're nearer to the day we'll die.
They know that too. Perhaps it's why they drink
And congregate in crowds to cheer and sing.
Is it denial? Do they really think
Time moving on is such a joyful thing?
I used to make an effort to be glad.
Not now. I stay home feeling old and sad.

Tallis's Canon

One of the things I'd like to do again
before I die is sing Tallis's Canon
in canon with other voices, using the words
written by the saintly Thomas Ken
for the use of the scholars of Winchester College:
Glory to thee my God this night
For all the blessings of the light.

It's years since I sang that hymn,
except to myself, or taught a child
to play it on the recorder.
I want to have it at my funeral,
not sung in canon – that would be
too complicated, and, anyway,
I wouldn't be there to join in the fun.

What a pity. I'd like everyone to imagine
how much I would have enjoyed
organising a churchful of people
into four parts, bringing them in
at the right moment, and singing my heart out:
Keep me, O keep me, King of kings,
Beneath thine own almighty wings.

Que Sera

The song was 'Que Sera, Sera'.
We sang and sang it in the car
Till Daddy called a halt.

Fatalistic and carefree –
That wasn't him. It isn't me –
Worriers to a fault,

Always keen to organise
The future, though the enterprise
Is sculpting water.

It goes on flowing anyhow.
Daddy has no future now
And mine is shorter.

As my last years cascade away
Moving faster every day,
The song comes back to me,

Saying you can't change what's coming,
Just let go and keep on humming
What will be, will be.

Every

Every ditch or stream or river the train crosses.
Every ploughed field, every row of trees.
Every square church tower in the distance.
Every minute of sunshine, every shadow.
Every wisp of cloud in the wide, blue, East Anglian sky.
Every day. Every day that's left.

UNCOLLECTED POEMS

— 2010–2017 —

Saint Hilda of Whitby: A Cantata

*commissioned by St Hilda's College, Oxford,
and set to music by Nicola LeFanu*

CHORUS

All who knew her called her Mother,
Abbess Hilda, full of grace.
Bishop, prince, monastic brother,
Loved the wisdom in her face,
Sought her counsel when in need,
Heard her teaching and gave heed.
All who knew her called her Mother,
Abbess Hilda, full of grace.

SOLO: BREGUSWITH (HILDA'S MOTHER)

I dreamed that my husband was taken away
And I could not find him. But in my dismay
I felt something under my robe – and I gazed
At a beautiful necklace of jewels that blazed
With a powerful light that shone from my hand
And filled with its splendour the whole of our land.

CHORUS

The dream came true. And Hilda was that light.
Her father murdered, she in exile learned
Of Christ and of his mysteries and yearned
To serve Him all her life, to serve the Lord
Until He called her home to her reward.

And thus she lived, so learned and devout
That godly Bishop Aidan sought her out
To rule, at first in one place, then another
As abbess of an order, Reverend Mother.
The dream came true. And Hilda was that light.

SOLO: HILDA

Here in this house of Whitby I decree
That all shall live in peace and charity.
No one shall be rich, no one in need,
All shall perform good works, and all must school
Themselves in Scripture, taking time to read,
To contemplate and learn. That is my Rule.

Above all, sisters, brothers, let us be
Together here in peace and charity.

CHORUS

But Abbess Hilda didn't think it wrong
To have a banquet, sing a merry song.
Everybody present at a feast
Would sing a song to entertain the rest.
A certain herdsman, Caedmon, was too shy –
He'd never learned to sing or versify.
Before it was his turn he would retire
To watch the oxen sleeping in the byre.
One night, something happened – something strange
And marvellous that caused his life to change.

SOLO: HILDA

Gentle Caedmon, put aside your fear
And speak to us who are assembled here

To listen. Tell us everything you told
The reeve this morning. Lift your eyes. Be bold.

SOLO: CAEDMON

Reverend Mother, someone stood
Beside me in my sleep and said
'Caedmon, sing to me'. And I
Replied, 'I cannot sing. That's why
I left the banquet.' 'Caedmon, sing
Of God creating everything.'

Mother, I sang:
> Now let us praise the Maker of heaven,
> The mighty Creator and his design.
> Let us praise the work of the Father of glory,
> The everlasting Lord, Author of all miracles,
> The Guardian of the human race,
> Who made the sky to be a roof
> And then the earth to be our home,
> Almighty God.

SOLO: HILDA

Caedmon, quiet, tongue-tied Caedmon, we
Conferred among ourselves and we agree
You are indeed inspired by heavenly grace.
And therefore you will take your vows and be
A brother in our learned company
And live as we do in this holy place.

CHORUS

Henceforward Caedmon spent his cloistered days
Learning Holy Scripture from the brethren.

The Word of God inspired the bard to raise
His voice in sweet harmonious songs of praise.

SOLO: HILDA

Help me, Lord, to live a holy life,
To be a peacemaker in times of strife.
When Christians differ, make us mindful of
Your teaching, and the healing power of love.

CHORUS

Caedmon died at last, a peaceful death,
Sleeping as he drew his final breath.

SOLO: BEGU (A NUN)

Hilda's holy soul was sorely tried
By years of suffering before she died:
Six years of burning fever.

I had a vision in my sleep last night
Of Hilda's soul ascending, bathed in light,
With angels guiding her towards the place
Where she would meet her Saviour face to face.

And after I awoke at break of day
They brought the news that she had passed away.

CHORUS

All who knew her called her Mother,
Abbess Hilda, full of grace.
Bishop, prince, monastic brother,
Loved the wisdom in her face,

Sought her counsel when in need,
Heard her teaching and gave heed.
All who knew her called her Mother,
Abbess Hilda, full of grace.

'Saint Hilda of Whitby' was performed in the University Church of St Mary the Virgin, Oxford on 18 February 2018 as part of the College's 125th anniversary celebrations. The text was later published as a booklet by the Jericho Press, Ely.

Teach Me

*'Who sweeps a room, as for thy laws,
Makes that and th'action fine.'*
— GEORGE HERBERT

The young man
smiling and singing
as he mops the floor
of King's Cross station
makes the action fine,
makes it beautiful,
makes me aware
in this unlikely place
of something in the world
we could call God.

Translation

This is what it has come to:
I am sitting at a desk
in a library in Wales

with your new poems
and a German dictionary.
There are glimpses

of something beautiful,
something profound,
but blurred, rarely precise.

For your decision
to abandon capital letters
I curse you, affectionately,

and I curse your language,
also with affection,
for the compound nouns

that compel me to look up
three different words
to understand one.

This is what it has come to:
I am seventy. I don't suppose
I'll ever see you again.

Haiku

Silly butterfly,
what are you doing indoors?
Look, there's the window.

On the Demise of Little Chef

reported in The Times, *27 May 2013*
(indebted to Wordsworth for verse 1)

He dwelt beside the busy ways
That lead from A to B
But now he is no more and, oh,
The difference to me.

Farewell, tubby little chap,
A pleb and not a toff.
The food was hot and quick and cheap.
You never ripped us off.

When I'm hungry on the road,
I don't want somewhere posh.
Whatever Giles Coren says,
I thank you for the nosh.

Some Little Chef restaurants survived for nearly a decade after their demise was announced, but all have now disappeared. Giles Coren is restaurant critic of *The Times*.

Roy

for Xanthe and Hector Lawson

Bad dog, Roy!
It's not a toy.
It's not a cat.
It's Wendy's hat.

But now, Roy, it's
Been chewed to bits.
And we know who
Did this. It's you.

That's why Dad
Is hopping mad
And why poor Mum
Is looking glum.

Listen, Roy.
Be a good boy.
Chew on a bone.
Leave hats alone.

UNCOLLECTED POEMS

— 2018–2023 —

The Aunts

for Eirwen Mabli Mackinnon

Who is coming? Do you know?
It's Aunty Jess and Aunty Jo.

Quickly let's clear up the mess
For Aunty Jo and Aunty Jess.

Wave your arms and say 'Hello'
To Aunty Jess and Aunty Jo.

Chatter, chatter, chatter – yes,
It's Aunty Jo and Aunty Jess.

They want to hold you. To and fro
From Aunty Jess to Aunty Jo

Until you've had enough, I guess
Of Aunty Jo and Aunty Jess.

But it's so quiet when they go -
Aunty Jess and Aunty Jo.

They love you very much. God bless
Aunty Jo and Aunty Jess.

A Poem

in response to 'Gift' by Czesław Miłosz

I read a poem today,
just nine lines long.

I tried to read another poem
but I couldn't – it had to be
the same poem over and over again.

Then I wrote this, my first poem
in months. What comes to mind
is a small chapel,
suddenly flooded with light.

On the Death of Archbishop Desmond Tutu

26 December 2021

Although I don't believe in the afterlife,
today I can't help but imagine
the Arch's arrival in Paradise.

As he emerges through the clouds,
his face radiant, the fanfare
of heavenly trumpets begins to swing

and all the angels are moving to the beat
as he dances, laughing with happiness,
into the arms of his Saviour.

Naga-Uta

Now I can't walk far
I head to the nearest park
where seventeen trees
are my enchanted forest.
In their dappled shade
I breathe slowly, touch the bark.
Somewhere a bird is singing.

The Beginning

for Aahva Benjamin Mackinnon Patel

None of us remembers the beginning:
the journey through a dark tunnel
to air and light, or our time
as a helpless baby.

When Aahva, two and three-quarters,
is the age I am now,
will he recall his obsession with vehicles,
how he loved to line up his toys
into a traffic jam, how the sighting
of a real-life bus or fire engine
was perfect happiness?

There he goes on his scooter,
faster and faster,
hurtling into the future.

The End

Not yet *sans everything*.
Thanks to my glasses, hearing aids, dental implant,
walking stick, inhalers, statins,
and carefully rationed painkillers,
I am glad to be alive
as I walk the last mile or two
through the valley of the shadow.

ACKNOWLEDGEMENTS

Jane Feaver played a crucial part in moving this project towards publication. Thanks to her, to Lavinia Singer also of Faber & Faber, and to Kate Burton of the publicity department, who has worked with me on my last two books and, fortunately, is still there to work on this one. Hamish Ironside lived up to his reputation as an ace typesetter. And thanks to Charles Walker and Olivia Martin of United Agents, who, as well as negotiating my book contracts, deal patiently with numerous permission requests and other fiddly bits of business on my behalf.

Thanks to Nicholas Garland for permission to reproduce his illustrations for *The River Girl*, and to Harry Oberländer for allowing the inclusion of his translated poems 'Sonnet of '68' and 'Lauda'.

Some of the uncollected poems in this volume previously appeared in one of the following publications: *Guardian, The Times, Spectator, Poetry Introduction 5* (Faber), *Waterstones Diary 1990, How to Become Ridiculously Well-Read in One Evening* (Penguin), *The Housman Society Journal, The Institute of Psychoanalysis Newsletter, Across the City* (Priapus Press), *Carnival of the Animals* (Walker Books), *Grand Piano*. 'The Beginning' and 'The End' were commissioned by We Present for a privately published anthology.

Index of Titles and First Lines

Titles are in *italic* type and first lines are in roman type.

1952 405
1972 414
19th Christmas Poem 180
30th December 231

A German dictionary on my knee 216
A little crowd had gathered in the square 349
A perfect white wine 351
A porcine aborigine 272
A talented young chimpanzee 318
A team of inspectors came round here today 265
A three-letter word beginning with f 309
ABC of the BBC, An 377
Absent Friends 410
Advertisement 18
Advice to Young Women 189
Aerial, The 147
Africans, The 337
After all these years 406
After Heine 388
After I heard that you had died 442
After Prague 245
After the Lunch 159
Afternoon, An 413
Ahead of My Time 207
All right, I'll tell you what I think 263
All who knew her called her Mother 461
All-Purpose Poem for State Occasions 6
Alone too much this week 155

Although I don't believe in the afterlife 475
An English meadow, early in the morning 91
An illuminated orb 404
An omelette doesn't want stirring 308
Anecdotes and jokes 451
Anne with an e and Ann without 357
Anniversary Poem, An 362
Another Christmas Poem 179
Another Unfortunate Choice 154
Another Valentine 364
April 352
Argument with Wordsworth, An 184
Art's whatever you choose to frame 448
As Sweet 150
At 3 a.m. 22
At 70 452
At Cathedral Mattins 303
At Christmas little children sing and merry bells jingle 165
At first I sent you a postcard 242
At first I'm startled by the sound of bicycles 231
At last, in spite of everything 396
At lunchtime I bought a huge orange 148
At New Place 432
At Stafford Services 341
At Steep 355
At the Poetry Conference 342
At the winter solstice 440
Attempt at Unrhymed Verse, An 317
Audience, The 367
Aunts, The 473
Autumn Haiku 306

Awake! for Morning on the Pitch
of Night 55

Bad dog, Roy! 470
Baggage 403
Bags 406
Ballad of an Office Romance 85
Because time will not run
backwards 11
Beginning, The 477
Being Boring 235
Bethlehem 397
Bloody Christmas, here again 179
Bloody men are like bloody
buses 186
Bloody Men 186
Boarders are better than
daygirls 332
Boarders 332
Born the King of Angels 324
Brahms Cradle Song 339
Bring in a tree, a young Norwegian
spruce 230
Budgie Finds His Voice 39
But a modulation to D flat minor 42
By the River 426
By the Round Pond 229

Calculations 418
Can someone make my simple wish
come true? 19
Cards to the very old 441
Cathedral Carol Service 323
Cathedral Limerick 304
Cento 448
Centuries of English verse 401
Christmas Cards 441
Christmas is coming 180
Christmas Life, The 230
Christmas Ornaments 322
Christmas Poem, A 165
Christmas Song, A 321
Christmas Triolet 395
Clearest of clear days 425
Closing the Anthology 219

Closing the anthology, I wonder if
it's time 219
Concerned Adolescent, The 194
Contented Poem, A 222
Cricketing Versions, The 177
Current Affairs 76

Daily Help 329
Damage to the Piano, The 402
Dead Sheep Poem 248
Dear George, although I do not share
your faith 437
Dear Organisers of Bard of the
Year 269
Dear Serious Novel 191
Defining the Problem 146
Deft, practised, eager 40
Depressed and disagreeable and
fat 246
Depression 65
Despite the piles of books and
papers 307
Die Farben der Bäume sind
schön 160
Differences of Opinion 325
Does She Like Word Games? 212
Don't ask him the time of day. He
won't know it 176
Don't see him. Don't phone or write
a letter 152
Don't want to go away. I never
do 391
Don't want to leave this place 256
Duffa Rex 43
Dutch Portraits 350

E Pericoloso Sporgersi 42
Each day I take a morning walk 252
Egg Cookery 308
Elegy for the Northern Wey 275
Ely 422
Emily Dickinson 15
End, The 478
Ending, An 256
Engineers' Corner 5

English Weather 209
Every ditch or stream or river the train crosses 458
Every 458
Everybody in this room is bored 270
Evidence 401
Exchange of Letters 191

Faint Praise 162
Faster and faster 236
Favourite 153
Fifty years have passed since we first met 412
Fine words won't turn the icing pink 16
Fire 71
Fireworks Poems 236
Flowers 145
For I will consider my lover, who shall remain nameless 28
For My Sister, Emigrating 170
Forty boys on benches with their quills 427
Forty-seven Words 387
From June to December 23

Giving Up Smoking 33
God and the Jolly Bored Bog-Mouse 47
God decided he was tired 39
God tried to teach Mouse how to sing 47
Going Away 66
Goldfish Nation 196
Good Christian men and women, let us raise a joyful shout 362
Grandmother 72
Grandmother, one tooth 72
Greek Island Triolets 259
Green Song, A 193
Grey mist and drizzle everywhere 218
Greydawn 340

Haiku ('A perfect white wine') 351

Haiku: Looking Out of the Back Bedroom Window without My Glasses 233
Haiku ('Silly butterfly') 468
Haiku: Willows 424
Hampshire Disaster, A 268
He couldn't be nicer if I were a king 220
He dwelt beside the busy ways 469
He has drawn lines 69
He tells her that the Earth is flat 262
He tells her that the Earth is flat 325
He Tells Her 262
He was a middle manager 85
He went. You said 245
He would refuse to put the refuse out 267
Health Advice 454
Health Scare, The 343
Here is a statue of a man who died 447
Here is Peter. Here is Jane. They like fun 9
Here We Are 421
Here we are 421
Here's a fine mess we got ourselves into 156
Higgledy-piggledy 15
homeless hammer, the 206
How like a sprinter 52
How shall we play this? We have all got votes 376
How sober was I 81
How to Deal with the Press 271

I ache 249
I always assumed it was French 224
I am a poet 172
I can't forgive you. Even if I could 146
I can't remember what you said about him 164
I cannot promise never to be angry 416
I don't believe in Heaven 388

I greet them with a friendly
    smile 303
I hardly ever tire of love or
    rhyme 185
I have been a non-smoker, now, for
    longer 418
I hope I can trust you, friends, not to
    use our relationship 347
I like *The Archers* only when it's
    got 377
I read a poem today 474
i spell it out on this fridge door 157
I stare at the ceiling 200
I think I am in love with A. E.
    Housman 154
I took her for my kind of person 390
I used to think all poets were
    Byronic 14
I worry about you 163
I Worry 163
I'll work, for there's new purpose in
    my art 34
I'm going to try and overcome my
    limitation 210
I'm living with Uncertainty and
    Fear 343
I've heard it on the radio 339
Idyll 234
If I don't know how to be thankful
    enough 232
If I Don't Know 232
If I went vegetarian 211
If I'm not sure, I can't say yes 360
If It Be Now 434
If it be now, 'tis not to come 434
If we were never going to die, I
    might 417
If you ask me 'What's new?', I have
    nothing to say 235
If you want to stay alive 454
In 'The Pied Piper of Hamelin' by
    Robert Browning 449
In a Clifftop Shelter at Falmouth 218
In April one seldom feels cheerful 12
In Demand 220

In London SE5 there lived a boy 279
In Memory of a Psychoanalyst 444
*In Memory of Dennis
    O'Driscoll* 442
*In Memory of Max Adrian 1903–
    1973* 435
In the pond 196
In the Rhine Valley 160
In the Wimpy Bar at Stafford
    services 341
Indeed 'tis true 54
It was a dream I had last week 61
It was the year 414
It wasn't you, it wasn't me 363
It wouldn't be a good idea 23
It's all because we're so alike 150
It's Christmas, season of wild
    bells 395
It's sad to think the actor never
    knew 435
It's very dark inside a book 222

January's grey and slushy 209
Jesus, Jesus! Who is on Jesus'
    side? 202
John Clare 255
John Clare, I cried last night 255
Journey, The 67

Keep saying this and don't
    forget 345
Keep Saying This 345
Kindness to Animals 211
King of the primeval avenues, the
    municipal parklands 43

Lantern Carol 440
Last year we went to Lissadell 354
Late home for supper 237
Lauda 215
Lavatory Attendant, The 41
Leaves. Leaves everywhere 306
Leaving 171
Legacy 168
Les Vacances 247

Let me massage your head 314
Let me not 53
Letter 155
Life tells us lies, inimitably 244
Limeglow of leaves 257
Limerick ('A talented young
  chimpanzee') 318
Lissadell 354
Little Donkey 439
Little Tribute to John Cage, A 446
Lonely Hearts 19
Loss 151
Love, love, love 190
Loving you is my favourite game 75
Lyric Poet, The 249

Macedonia 1987 349
Magnetic 157
Making Cocoa for Kingsley Amis 61
Maman et Papa au bord de la
  mer 247
Manifesto 34
March 2013 423
Marriage, The 428
Married at eighteen to a pregnant
  bride 428
Melancholy's grape: today I've bitten
  it 342
Memorial 415
Men and Their Boring
  Arguments 187
Men Talking 451
Message 32
Mr Strugnell 37
Month of May, The 353
Months ago I dreamed of a tulip
  garden 276
Motorway Music 396
Mozart in the Shopping Centre 305
Mummy's cousin Evelyn 335
Mummy's working-class
  relations 338
My computer humming 446
My father must have bought it
  secondhand 431

My Father's Shakespeare 431
My Favourite Game 75
My Funeral 347
My glass can't quite persuade me
  I am old 436
My glass shall not 50
My heart has made its mind
  up 161
My love got in the car 238
My Lover 28
My next project 77
My schoolfriend Roz, who died
  twenty years ago 410
My sister 73
My true love hath my heart and I
  have hers 83
Mystery, A 250

Naga-Uta ('Clearest of clear
  days') 425
Naga-Uta ('Now I can't walk
  far') 476
Names 169
Narrative 46
New Regime, The 166
New Season 167
New Year 455
Next summer? The summer
  after? 171
Nine-Line Triolet 156
No coats today. Buds bulge on
  chestnut trees 167
Noises in the Night 188
None of us remembers the
  beginning 477
Not from the stars 49
Not only marble 51
Not the one he planted but its
  'scion' 432
Not yet *sans everything* 478
Now I can't walk far 476
Now, children, this fine animal is
  called the pianist 312
Nursery Rhyme (as it might have
  been written by T. S. Eliot), A 11

Nursery Rhyme (as it might have been written by William Wordsworth), A 10

O Come, All Ye Faithful 324
Of fitness and vitality I am not the epitome 452
Oh no, not him, sir. He's no good 311
Oh, never say 80
Oh, once I was a policeman young and merry 7
Old Boys' Day 359
Omo 334
On a Country Bus 158
On a Photograph of the Archbishop of Canterbury 450
On a Train 240
On Finding an Old Photograph 20
On Learning the Correct Pronunciation of the Name of a Poetic Form 224
On Sonnet 18 429
On Sonnet 22 436
On the Death of Archbishop Desmond Tutu 475
On the Demise of Little Chef 469
On the flyleaf 241
On the platform where the school train left 66
On Waterloo Bridge, where we said our goodbyes 159
Once I'm Dead 346
Once I'm dead, I won't mind being dead 346
One cold day, emerging 334
One Day 419
One day, my love, the good times will be over 419
One green bottle 193
One man on his own can be quite good fun 187
One of the things I'd like to do again 456
Orange, The 148

Orb 404
Our planet spins around the sun 194

People are always quoting that and all of them seem to agree 184
People say, 'What are you doing these days? What are you working on?' 250
People tell you all the time 317
Pianists 312
Pick up the phone before it is too late 32
Poem, A 474
Poem about Jesus, A 438
Poem Composed in Santa Barbara 173
Poem for L 307
Poem from a Colour Chart of House Paints 257
Poem on the Theme of Humour, A 269
Poet's Song, The 174
Policeman's Lot, A 7
Postcard Poem 221
Postcards 242
Present 241
Probably 360
Proverbial Ballade 16

Que Sera 457

A Reading 270
Reading Berryman's Dream Songs at the Writers' Retreat 251
Reading Scheme 9
Reflections on a Royalty Statement 182
Rehearsal, A 376
Reunion 412
Revenge 77
Riddle 309
River Girl, The 91
Roger Bear's Football Poems 199
Roger Bear's Philosophical Pantoum 200

Rondeau Redoublé 31
Row upon row of grey heads 359
Roy 470

Saint Hilda of Whitby:
    A Cantata 461
School outing, 1960: Romeo 433
Score 68
Seeing you will make me sad 348
Seeing You 348
Serious Concerns 210
Shadows of lamp posts 68
Shakespeare at School 427
Shall I compare 82
She left two Premium Bonds 168
She likes sonnets but she doesn't like
    poems 212
She was Eliza for a few weeks 169
She'll urge you to confide.
    Resist 271
Shorter Version of Wordsworth's
    Immortality Ode, A 84
Silly butterfly 468
Sisters 73
Sitter, The 246
Sixty-one and on a diet 344
Sixty-one 344
Size isn't everything. It's what you
    do 162
Slumped on a chair, his body is an
    S 41
'So long as men can breathe and eyes
    can see' 429
So Much Depends 164
Some men never think of it 145
Some More Light Verse 149
Some pupils here have special
    needs 358
Some socks are loners 264
Sometimes, instead of a farthing 405
Song 238
Sonnet ('A German dictionary on my
    knee') 216
Sonnet of '68 243
Sorrow of Socks, The 264

South Bank Poetry Library, London,
    The 310
Spared 363
Special Needs 358
Sporty People 390
Sprinkle the air around you 207
Squirrel and the Crow, The 252
Stars 361
Statue, A 447
Stickleback Song, The 265
Stress 267
Strugnell in Liverpool 44
Strugnell Lunaire 205
Strugnell's Bargain 83
Strugnell's Evangelical Songs 202
Strugnell's Haiku 57
Strugnell's Royal Wedding
    Poem 313
Strugnell's Rubáiyát 55
Strugnell's Sonnets 48, 79
Sunday Morning 327
Sunday morning. Things get
    tense 327
Sunset at Widemouth Bay 71

Tallis's Canon 456
Teach Me 466
Teacher's Tale, The 279
Team Spirit 311
Ted Williams Villanelle, The 261
Thanks for putting up with me 387
Thaw 70
The aerial on this radio broke 147
The birds are singing loudly
    overhead 352
The book I've been reading 240
The cherry blossom 57
The children's favourite. We
    had 439
The choir sings 'Grant us thy
    salvay-see-oan' 304
The day he moved out was
    terrible 151
The day is so still 426
The expense of spirits 48

The fat boy in the seat across the aisle 158
The hotter the star, the bluer it shines 361
The journey was difficult at first 67
The lady takes *The Times* and *Vogue* 18
The mice attacked the Holy Family 322
The month of May, the merry month of May 353
The nation rejoices or mourns 6
The poets talk. They talk a lot 173
the room contains no sound 22
the sick umbrella underneath the council chamber 206
The silver moon pours down her light 205
The sky was dark, the garden gnomes were still 46
The skylark and the jay sang loud and long 10
The song was 'Que Sera, Sera' 457
The two of them are sitting on the bed 413
The uproar's over, and the calls to fight 243
The winter's going on and on 423
The worst row we two ever had concerned 430
The year has died. Another year is born 455
The young man 466
There are so many kinds of awful men 31
There isn't much cricket in *Hamlet* either 177
There stands a church in Bethlehem today 397
There's not a Shakespeare sonnet 33
They became angels. And their wings could lift 215
They used to be delivered by the milkman 223
They've given me a number 182

Thirteen Ways of Curing a Headache 314
This fly believes I'm dead 259
This is a pleasant library. I'd enjoy every minute 310
This is the moment 275
This is what it has come to 467
This morning we saw sheepskin rugs 248
'This was Mr Strugnell's room,' she'll say 37
Those of us who are not important enough 323
Three cheers for Spurs! 199
Three scruffy teenagers 305
Tich Miller wore glasses 21
Tich Miller 21
Timekeeping 237
To a mite 84
To find myself in tears is a surprise 350
To My Husband 417
Today we are obliged to be romantic 364
Traditional Prize County Pigs 272
Translation 467
Travel Sonnet 391
Tree, The 420
Triolet 14
Tulips 276
Tumps 176
Two Ann(e)s 357
Two Cures for Love 152
Two smart porters carry luggage on 403

Uncertainty of the Poet, The 172
Uncle Bill 338
Under trees 70
Upheavals 408
Usquebaugh 40

Valentine 161
Variation on a Lennon and McCartney Song 190

Variation on Belloc's 'Fatigue' 185
Villanelle for Hugo Williams, A 356
Visitors from Africa! 337
Vow, A 416

waking early 44
Waste Land Limericks 12
Watch the ball and do your thing 261
We had to leave our home. We travelled here 420
We loved each other, you and I 217
We make more fuss of ballads than of blueprints 5
We stumble down the sloping path 355
We thought our little city got its name 422
We used it every day 340
We'll be in our garden on a summer evening 234
Wendy went a-swimming. It was dreadful 251
What can I say? I'd like to be polite 356
What I Think 263
What's that amazing 233
When fire engulfed the headquarters 268
When I find myself feeling sorry for the wrong people 438
When I got home from Aunty Bob's funeral 415
When I started to write as a very young man 174
When I was home in the holidays 408
When in disgrace 79
When they ask me, 'Who's your favourite poet?' 153

When will the miners go back underground? 76
When you're a spinster of forty 189
Where art thou Muse? Phone home. I need you here 313
Where Do You Get Your Ideas From? 223
Where's a Pied Piper When You Need One? 449
Who is coming? Do you know? 473
Why are men so good at sleeping? 188
Why is the baby crying 321
Will they do this, I wonder 221
Willows white with frost 424
Women's Merchant Navy, The 335
Word before Sleep, A 244
Word-Watching 69
Worst Row, The 430
Wreath for George Herbert, A 437

Yalding, 1912. My father 20
Yes, I agree. We'll pull ourselves together 166
You and I 217
You can barely see 402
You have to try. You see a shrink 149
You lie, snail-like, on your stomach 65
You see an archbishop out jogging in shorts 450
You seem so small 329
You watch yourself. You watch the watcher too 229
You're not allowed to wonder if it's true 328
You're Not Allowed 328
You've left with me 170
Young Love 433
Your funeral. And on the day 444